THE C.J. DENN
COLLECTION

THE C.J. DENNIS COLLECTION

from his 'forgotten' writings

Edited by Garrie Hutchinson

Lothian
BOOKS

Thomas C. Lothian Pty Ltd
11 Munro Street, Port Melbourne, Victoria 3207

First published 1987
This edition first published 1999

National Library of Australia
Cataloguing-in-Publication data:

Dennis, C.J. (Clarence James), 1876–1938
The C.J. Dennis collection : from his "forgotten" writings

ISBN 0 73440053 5

I. Hutchinson, Garrie, 1949– . II. Title.

A828.2

Cover: painting by Clarice Beckett
Printed by Griffin Press Pty Limited

CONTENTS

Illustrations by Sam Wells, Alex Gurney and Percy Leason accompanied the original work.

A PRINCE OF WRITERS

Only one bloke has been obliged to become poet laureate of Australia. C. J. Dennis. He once said that he would give up all other triumphs in his country's service if he could write his country's songs. And in a way he did — not pompous, jingoistic anthems but disarmingly simple songs of ordinary Australians.

People like the Sentimental Bloke, Ginger Mick, Doreen, Digger Smith and Rose of Spadgers — spoke in a language that Australians have always understood, whatever its literary origins.

Apart from his famous character sequences, Dennis wrote literally thousands of other songs — poems — stories — in newspapers and magazines. That work, whether written for the moment or in a more considered way, also deserves appreciation by the legion of Den's admirers.

This collection is mainly concerned with the poems and articles Dennis published in *The Melbourne Herald*, where he was invited by Sir Keith Murdoch to become a daily verse-journalist in 1922. Dennis held this unique position, against odds of ill-health and the nature of the job itself, until his death in 1938. The only break was when he was more than usually ill, between May 1924 and February 1927.

In the 4,000-odd uncollected poems and prose pieces that he wrote in those times, there are ordinary things, and things so ephemeral that they are meaningless today. There are thoughts about people and events that are as old hat as the topper. On the other hand there are hundreds of poems and pieces that deserve to be rescued. Many of them are published, for the first time in fifty years, here.

They might appear slight sometimes, for part of Dennis' genius was that he wrote for ordinary people, with humour and a self-deprecating humanness that allows him, and the characters he invents for himself, to live and make us smile.

An effort has been made not to repeat the material in *Random Verse*, a selection made by Dennis' wife under the name Margaret Herron, published in 1952.

* * * *

Clarence Michael James Dennis, with a christening name of Stanislaus, was known as 'Den'. He was born in Auburn, South Australia of Irish parents.

He was born with the gift of the gab and was soon in love with words — the sound of them, the feel of them. He couldn't resist starting magazines. The habit began at school.

And grog. Den liked a drink.

Den left school at 17 and in 1893 had a job as a junior clerk in a stock and station agents in Adelaide. He is reputed to have been fired for reading H. Ryder Haggard, author of *King Solomon's Mines* and *She* at his desk. He went back to Laura, and worked as a solicitor's clerk, as well as barman at the nearby Beetaloo Hotel. The next few years saw him in many occupations, besides that of writing. His first verse was published in Laura in 1895, and in 1898 he first worked as a journalist, spending a year on the staid Adelaide weekly, *The Critic*.

In 1899 he was back in Laura. Looking back on his life at the time he said, 'The old man spoiled me. I lived the life of an idle young fool. I did as I liked and I learned to drink.'[1]

He then went to Broken Hill for 18 months working as a 'miner, carpenter, railway construction labourer, photographer's canvasser and insurance agent.' He rejoined *The Critic* in 1901, first contributed to the *Bulletin* in 1903, and then started *The Gadfly* with the 16 year old A. E. Martin. The first issue of this satirical magazine appeared on 14 February 1906. Dennis contributed 200 pieces under various noms de plume. It was a paper that continually teetered on the edge of bankruptcy.

Sing a song of sixpence.
A pocket full of hope.
Four and twenty printers' bills
In an envelope.
When the bills were opened
The staff began to cry:
Wasn't that an awful thing
To set before the 'Fly'!

The Gadfly closed in 1909, but Dennis had already left for Melbourne at the end of 1907, in search of more and better paid writing work. He ended up in 1908 in a tent at Toolangi, north of Melbourne, writing and sending things by post. He might as well have been back o' Bourke.

Den first saw Toolangi, in the Great Dividing Range about 80km northwest of Melbourne, in 1908 when he was shown the district by Hal Waugh, the painter. They lived in two tents: The Hall of Hal and The Den of Den. He wrote the *Australaise* in the tent for The *Bulletin's* national song competition and was awarded a prize.

'Blessed' or 'blooming' were officially allowable in this great anthem, but other words have been known to have been used. Den is the only poet in literary history to find a satisfactory rhyme for Australia(r).

Joy is — fleetin',
  Life is — short.
Wot's the use uv wastin' it
  All on — sport?

Hitch yer — tip-dray
  To a — star.
Let yer — watchword be
  "Australi- — -ar!"

After a few months in the tent Den moved into an abandoned timber getters hut and, except for a trip to Sydney, a honeymoon in Cairns, renovations and extentions and the use of a flat in Collins Street, Melbourne, he stayed for the rest of his life.

Den lived like a hermit in the mountains, writing and sending poems off to the *Bulletin*, including the first *Songs of the Sentimental Bloke* in 1909. Not much of a life and not, according to some new friends he met in 1913, as much as his genius demanded. He luckily met Robert Croll, who was walking through the hills, and through him John Garibaldi Roberts, who lived at Kallista. 'Garry' Roberts (whom Den called Dad) was an accountant and later manager of the Melbourne Tramway & Omnibus Company. He had a few old trams on his property and Den was allocated one as a studio.

Den, under the influence of encouragement, new literary friends, food, another place to stay and write and a small 'pension' (which depended for payment on a weekly production) wrote like an angel. Appropriately enough he finished *The Sentimental Bloke* in the tram over the next couple of years.

* * * *

Dennis' reputation of course rests firmly on the shoulders of *The Bloke*, whose Songs have been continuously in print since 1915. Someone once added up the number of copies of Den's books printed in various editions, and got close to a million.

Banjo Paterson was asked by Den, and the Banjo's normally perspicacious and watchful publisher George Robertson in 1927, to write a bush 'something' along the lines of *The Sentimental Bloke*, and was given a £100 to go with it. Despite this inducement Banjo couldn't make it work and felt obliged to give the money back. Henry Lawson introducing *The Bloke* in 1915 said, 'I dips me lid, and stands aside.'

The Bloke, and his kindred works, *The Moods of Ginger Mick, Digger Smith* and *Doreen* are still alive and well, even if in a very different Australia than the one Den knew or imagined. And even if the romantically grubby world of Little Lon.[2] and later the idyllic cherry farm in the hills never really existed except in the minds of Den and us. Who cares. They should have.

* * * *

His first book, the first edition of *Backblock Ballads*, was published by E. W. Cole in 1913, and included some of *The Bloke*. It wasn't a great success. In 1914 Den visited Sydney and wrote for the *Australian Worker* and Labor Party election paper *The Call*. War was declared in August and Den returned to Melbourne in September and lived at the Roberts' house in Hawthorn, then at Kallista. In January 1915 after talking to some Labor MPs he got a job in the Navy Office in Melbourne for £3 a week. He was 'on the chain' and boarded in Camberwell. The next year he became secretary to Labor Senator E. J. Russell.

In 1916 he had a serious accident — he was hit by a tram, adding to his bronchial, asthmatic, booze and work-affected physiology.

All this was nothing compared to the publication of *Songs of a Sentimental Bloke*, by George Robertson of Angus and Robertson in 1915. It had been turned down by a least two Melbourne publishers as too 'coarse' in language. It has since sold over 285,000 copies, surely the biggest sale any poet, not excluding Banjo Paterson, has had in this country.

The Bloke has also been recorded numerous times and been turned successfully into three musicals, the latest in 1985.

Den was a success all of a sudden, making a bit of coin — £900 from the first edition of *The Bloke*. He followed it up with the Digger's second favourite, *The Moods of Ginger Mick*.

He married Olive 'Biddy' Herron in 1917 and, after a honeymoon in Cairns, renovated and extended the shack at Toolangi, and never left it again for long. He called it 'Seaview' at first, though it would take Superman or a comic to see the sea, and then 'Arden' as the garden grew.

In 1917 he published *Doreen* (which had first appeared in the *Bulletin* in 1909), and *The Glugs of Gosh*, an elaborate satire on suburbia, bureaucracy and free-trade. *Digger Smith* followed in 1918, and the last of the 'Bloke' books, *Rose of Spadgers* in 1924.

* * * *

Den began to work at the *Herald*, Melbourne, as staff writer/poet in 1922, when he was 46 and easily the most successful writer of any sort alive in Australia. It was the sort of thing that happened on Melbourne newspapers then — especially one with an eye to gathering the best writers and artists available to the stable and dominating the popular morning and evening markets. Percy Leason, Vance Palmer and Will Dyson were all gathered to the fold during this time.

Den wrote exclusively, and almost daily for the *Herald* until his death in 1938. During his 16 years in harness as the staff poet, his only absences were through illness. Just about a third of his working life was then taken up with the very particular craft of writing poetry (verse if you like), and his own special brand of prose in a popular newspaper.

Den's bibliographer, Ian McLaren, has tracked down over 3000 items written by Den in those years, an extraordinary amount of work for anyone even a journalist.

What is impressive about the achievement is not just the quantity of works but the quality of Den's imagination. Anyone who has ever attempted to write a column for a newspaper, purely from one's own resources, can only admire the professionalism as well as envy the craft. It's not simply like reporting the news of the day (though from time to time Den reflects on that), it's having to invent the news.

Den tried a variety of tricks over the years. He began with a genuine column that would be recognisable in today's newspapers called *The Mooch of Life*. This contained paragraphs culled and commented on from the news, odd spots, comments, bits of dialogue, little plays and poems.

After a bit he invented Ben Bowyang, that rural filosofer and spelin reformer, who wrote from the bush and was occasionally arst by the editor to attend a Test Match or the resslin in Melbun.

The Bowyang spelin was sometimes corrected, and he was forced to arst the editer if he 'wud arst yure printer not to maik so manny mistaiks when e is puttin my ritin into tipe. wots the good of ritin good articels when it gits orl ful of misprince.'

Occasionally *The Sentimental Bloke* was brought back for important moments such as Anzac Day and Remembrance Day. Den, the poet of the Diggers, wrote something for them every year.

He wrote to celebrate important days in the year's passing. The beginning of the football season, Christmas, the Cup, the Show and summer holidays. He could always rely on Politicians and Poms, flannelled fools and flappers, our language and theirs, war and peace to turn up a bit of grist for his mill.

He invented long running tasks for himself: 30 Country Towns and five Country Roads, thirteen Political Personalities, twelve Melbourne Streets, some fifty Bush Birds all of which plus some other things were published in his last book *The Singing Garden*.

There are 29 Old Town Types, a dozen Ditties of Debunk and 51 Epistles from Ab, who was another bush letter writer. Den reported the reflections of a great variety of characters — Percy Podgrass, The Bald Monologist, George Applecrop, Bobby J., Miss Mix and Pete Parraday.

A few glimpses of Den's facility with words have been recorded.

> During the time he was magazine editor of the *Herald* Den had a flat in Collins Street and returned to the Hills (his little car laden with commodities) only at weekends. His working day began with an editorial conference. That over, he would start a pipe and a kettle going and begin a search for verse ideas amid the clatter of crockery. Occasionally one or other of the four or five fellows who drifted in to join the tea-party would contribute an idea. More often he dug it out for himself. Then, alternately sipping tea and puffing at his pipe, he would begin to rhyme. He never seemed to bustle, but he always got the verses through on time. Meanwhile, as long as any hot water remained the tea sipping and the pipe puffing continued.

Another factor in the Dennis technique was to have a number of flower filled vases in the room. If the blooms faded and no others were immediately available he always insisted on retaining the old ones. He used to say that he would rather have faded flowers than none at all, and he defended that queer taste against all comers.

Tea, tobacco and flowers — those were Dens supports in the days when he was both a topical verse writer and a magazine editor.[3]

Den's wife wrote later:

> Looking back down the years, that [Den's move back to the city in 1922] was the unwisest thing we ever did. The city was no place for a man of Den's temperament. A column of verse daily was strenuous for a man who had been out of harness so long. Temptations were many, and at times he would give way to his weakness and have to go into hospital.

Den's weakness was, like Henry Lawson's and many a journalist, the grog. The great black and white artist, Will Dyson, a mate of Den's said of him to Den's wife:

> 'There were only two things that prevented him from becoming a monk. One was his aptitude for rhyming, the other — his appetite for —' he glanced across at Den, who was sitting opposite, 'his appetite' he finished lamely.[4]

Den wrote a little poem about this 'appetite' on the occasion of a judge while sentencing a man for driving under the influence, saying there were degrees of intoxication.

HIC!
He is 'slightly elevated' if he 'Hics',
And the fine might possibly be 2/6.
If he drivels silly rot.
Why, the fellow's plainly 'shot'.
And he's 'blithered' if an argument he picks.

If he staggers he is 'stonkered,' 'sozzled', 'stung':
If his voice is rather thick
He's unquestionably 'shick'.
But he's 'blotto' if he can't control his tongue.

He is 'potty' if he talks a lot of 'bunk',
In other words, he's 'soused', 'inked', 'molar', 'sunk'.
But this test most rarely misses:
If the constable he kisses.
Why, it's obvious the fellow must be drunk.[5]

Mrs Dennis sometimes had to hold Den's head under a cold tap in order for him to meet a deadline — which for an evening paper like the *Herald* is quite early in the day. On the other hand he knocked out four six-line verses on the death of G. K. Chesterton (one of Chesterton's mottos: If a thing is worth doing, it's worth doing badly) in twenty minutes right on deadline.

The poem about Chesterton, written on 16 June, 1936 might serve Dennis as well.

It begins:

And so this hearty jester ends his day
And passes, with an ale-mug in his hand.
Leaving us better since he passed this way
Who did so love his jest, his God, his land:
And, as the last quip on his still lip dies,
A chuckle echoes down the further skies.

And ends:

We watch him strolling thro' Elysian ways,
Half smiling as he goes to know his fate:
A word for Gabriel of the clear, straight gaze,
A jape for Peter smiling at the gate:
Then sudden, reverent knees pressed to the sod.
A jester unashamed before his God.

Still an evening paper gives a man with a taste ample opportunity — even after tobacco, tea and flowers had caused the day's work to be done. As it happens he gave Melbourne up for Toolangi, exclusively, in 1932.

Dennis' work in the *Herald* was a disappointment to those Australians who prefer the Dennis who was a savage social critic in his days with the *Gadfly*, the *Bulletin,* the *Worker*. It is said that he 'gradually took on the attitudes of the newspaper which employed him,' which attitudes were conservative and anti-Labor.[6]

The Labor Party had been Den's patron, finding him jobs when he needed them during the war. Later he turned against it. That seems to be the major charge. To half the population Den simply showed common sense, and in the 1980s a good many more would understand how a political party, anxious for office, can apparently desert its supporters.

Den put it this way:

They may be duds or they may be drones,
Or legislators heaven-sent.
But the ALP for all atones
When it gets them into Parliament.

In the middle of the depression, he wrote:

> Seven hungry Treasurers
> With sad and hopeless eyes
> Have tired of late to conjugate
> The verb 'economise'.
> And seven harried Treasurers,
> With figures on the brain.
> Lost in the maze, a chorus raise:
> With this sad refrain:
>
> Oh what about the promises?
> On those our public dotes,
> What about the promises
> That used to win the votes—
> The bonus and the subsidy
> That pave the way to fame?
> Oh, what about the promises
> That kept us in the game?[7]

But it wasn't just politicians in general. He wrote during the 1929 Election campaign against the Labor Party, especially the 'radicals' like Jack Lang, frequently Premier of NSW. He spoke of the nice Dr Jekylls, the nice front men, like Scullin and the 'strangely quiet' Lang, who was Den's Mr Hyde. Six stanzas of invective concluded like this: 'Suppose I cast a Labor vote — who will be on my side. The Labor Dr Jekyll or the Labor Mr Hyde?'[8]

Such nasty naivete is hard to forget, but not unexpected. To think that Den became conservative is to pretend that Dennis was less complex than he was, a parallel belief to the one that in *The Bloke, Ginger Mick, The Glugs of Gosh* he was a simple rhymester, unaware of the social and philosophical content of his work. As with the technical poetical tasks he was meeting and solving, he knew precisely what he was doing.

Dennis held several things constant in his life. He wanted to make a living as a writer in Australia, and more especially as a poet. He is perhaps the only one who ever has achieved that, but he was always anxious about money.

Dennis was a nationalist from start to finish, with all the baggage entailed in that notion in this country, especially in his time. He was a sentimentalist about the bush, the bush workers, Anzac and war, at the same time as seeing the wasteful hell of war. He was always on the side of the Digger and profoundly in their debt for what they sacrificed, their humour in the face of pointlessness, their Australian-ness in a foreign cause.

He was a protectionist, apprehensive of cheap foreign goods and cheap foreign labour. He thought this meant Asian hordes sometimes. He was sympathetic to the Aborigines without ever having anything to do with any of them. He made fun of the Chinese, American (white and black) and Poms (especially Dukes). He was also deeply affected by England without ever going there. King, Shakespeare, Language, Poets, Parliament. He was an unreconstructed romantic about women.

He was deeply concerned with the Australian language, as she was spoke, and as she was wrote, protecting her from the depredations of the schoolmasterly pedant, especially those in England. He disliked the modernist movement in poetry.

He was a sceptical barracker for football and cricket. He loved swaggies, all birds, flowers, ants, wombats, farms and farmers, the bush. He was amused by the city and hated small towns, small minds and suburbia.

And he never took orders from anyone about what he should write about, in the *Herald* or anywhere else. It was all his own work. In the end Den's love of Australians and Australian things far outweighs his cranky politics.

* * * *

I would like to thank the staff and machinery at the Herald & Weekly Times library, the Baillieu Library Special Collections and the LaTrobe Library for their assistance with this book. Most of all I am, as are all Den's mates, indebted to Ian McLaren for his astounding industry and accuracy in preparing the C. J. Dennis bibliographies.

Garrie Hutchinson

1. Margaret Herron, *Down the Years*, Hallcraft, Melbourne 1963 p13.
2. Little Lonsdale Street, Melbourne.
3. A. R. Chisholm *The Making of a Sentimental Bloke*, Georgian House, Melbourne 1946, p122, quoting a 'front line observer'.
4. Herron p64.
5. *Herald*, July 5 1928.
6. Geoffrey Hutton. *C. J. Dennis*, Premier's Department Victoria 1976 p42.
7. *Herald*, August 14, 1930.
8. *Herald*, October 4, 1929 — Labor won and later the Langites were expelled from the ALP. Den seems to have been unrepentant.

RESPITE

I am off and away to the hills today,
To the hills with the sky behind,
Where never sign of a metric line
Shall mar my piece of mind.
Where the clear stream goes and babbles prose
With never a hint of time,
Far from the curse of a tyrant verse
And rhyme, rhyme, rhyme.

I shall sing no thing with a rhythmic swing
And a meaning somewhat dim:
I shall hunt no more for the verse-form hoar
Or the shy, shy synonym:
Where all day long the birds sweet song
Knows naught of metric lore.
Where the wind-blown tree sways jerkily
And couplets are no more.

Soft shall I pass o'er rhymeless grass
A free unfettered man,
Where the old bush road hints at no ode
And the skyline does not scan:
Where the foolish beat of my tramping feet
Is the only sound to mar
The peace of those who cleave to prose
In the timbered hills afar.

But I shall not walk: I shall not talk
Lest I should lapse in rhyme:
But safe and free from prosody,
I'll have a high old time.
Oh, my hopes are high: my pen's laid by
And my mind is on the shelf.
And if you long for a Christmas song.
Go write the thing yourself.

Herald, December 23, 1927.

FROM THE BUSH

FLAVOR OF TADPOLES

gunns gully
april 18

dere frend

wot are you quinchin yer thurst with these days.

we ave giv up avin meels in gunns gully more or less sins the criks ave been runnin low we git enuf soluds in our drinkin warter to satisfy a gluttin.

i mus say i aint mutch shuk on the flaver of tad poles. they are a akwired tast like wombats. but sum of the warter beedles is a bit tasty.

bil smith tels me that the warter wots left in is crick is orl full of miskeeter riglers so is missis boyles orl the warter befor they drinks it. that seems to me like a lotter rot becos as i tels him i cant tast no difrince between boyled miskeeters an ror miskeeters so e is only wastin is time.

this ere drout wether as corsed bil to chu things over a bit in is mind an e as wurked out a bit of a theery. e puts it to me the uther day an arsts me dont i think its feezible.

bils ideer is that a man can giv up avin anythink if e only takes an nocks it orf gradjil. take worter bil sez. if a man drunk less an less of it evry day til e got isself down to a cupler tee spoons ful bine by 'e cud nock that orf gradjil til e cud liv without anny worter at tall. an e cud teech is orses an cows an crops to do the same bit by bit an then it wudent mater if we never got no more rane.

i tells bil it mite be a bit risky tryin the theery with worter fer a start. as e wus jist on is way parst the pub i pints out it mite be a good ideer to ave a ixperimint with beer fer a trile.

but bil sez no e sez is theery aint feezible at tall when it cums to nessyserrys. an e wus so narked about it e fergot to arst me if i wus going is way.

i see be the pappers that this ere noo darncin craz seems to be sending em orl dippy in ingland an amerika. darncin fer ours an days without stopin. it looks to me like they wus going cleen orf ther panikins an we are startin to git a bit nervis abowt it up ere.

you no wot yung fokes is in the bush abowt darncin. if that craz wus oncet to git a holt up ere amung the yung peepil the ole lanscap wud jist be a mask of wirlin figgers nite an day an no wurk did.

when we begun notisin that the yung fokes wus takin a intrest in this darncin nonsens in the pappers me an bil an ole pete airey an a few uthers puts our eds together an tries to start a sorter counter atak like burnin a fire brake agin a bush fire. but we deden ave mutch sugsess.

furst orf we got up a long distans cow milkin compytishun. but yung erb airey got a gramyfone out in the yard an starts milkin to a jaz choon an that aint no good to a cows tits.

as it was my cow i calls the compytishun orf. an the yung fokes ad a impromchoo darnce til ole airey dun in the gramyfone with a ax.

nex time we trid a non stop fern cuttin compytishun. but a blok cum along with a tin wisle and after e ad plaid a wals choon fer a bit the ole thing looked like it wus going to be a fi asko.

as they wus cutting in my paddick i slips the blok with the wisle a cupler bob to pla a ilan fling.

they cut abowt 3 akers of ferns an a lotter ther legs before the wislers wind giv out. so i never dun so bad orl kinserned.

torkin of the drowt ther wus a city blok stayin at ole aireys lars weak with a grate sens of umer.

wun mornin e cum out in is pijamers with a towl an a tooth brush an a biter sope an sed e thort w wud ave a barth.

they orl neer dide larfin at im but e never seen the jok.

airey tells im why ther aint enuf warter to spar to barth a blofly an e better ave a rub down with a bag sam as they dun an thank even it never raned bags or e cudent ave that.

then the blok got snarky an sez thanks orl the sam but e perfered to stop dirty.

hoppin you are the sam

yours truly

Ben Bowyang

BOWYANG IS CANDID

dere frend

wel i ope yous got back to town safe after spendin yer little olyday with us up ere.

i wisht yous cud ave staid longer than a cupler days becos ther was a lotter things i was ichin to tell yer but i never got a chanct.

mine i aint slingin orf at yer abowt torkin to mutch or annythink like that becos owever umbel me lot in life i opes i nos me manners. but you musent think that becos us peepil in the bush is good lisners we dont want to get a word in egways sumtimes.

them lekshers was reel interestin wot you give us on the need of sity parks, an over crowdin tranes, an the roodnes of tram kinduckters or the bad inflooens of movin pitchers. it was al reel entertainin but to tel you the hones trooth i was ankshus to ave a bit of a wurd with you abowt rottin rodes an pertater blite an 1 thing an nuther but i diden seam to git no chanct. but i aint slingin orf or nothink like that.

you an me as been good frends now for a fare number of yeers an i no that we alwiz takes wot wun anuther sez in good part an the spirut in wich it is ment. plane tork between frends is alwiz the best i sez if yous want to remane frends. cander pays in the long run as the sayin is.

so I no yous ull take it in good part an not rekin ime slingin orf when i points out 1 or 2 littel brakes yous made when yous was up ere.

frinstans when yure misses sez to bil smith that e wurked is bullicks so ard that e never seemed to ave time to milk the pore things ther wasent no need fer er to go sower just becos bil larfed. i no bils got a narsty sorter larf but it cums frum is art an ort to be took in the same spirut as it is ment an thats kinely like.

I aint sayin nothin abowt yous ixpectin ot barths evry mornin becos I spose its jist a abit yous git like drinkin an terback. if we ad knowed sity peepil needed washin so mutch weed ave put on a cupler karaseen tins of warter for yous. but when yure missus starts inquirin fer servyets at the diner table she deden orter ave looked down er nose when we giv er a ankerchef. it was a clean ankerchef annyway. an this ouse dont run to servyets or finger boles eether an you got to tak us as you find us. but dont you go thinkin ime slingin orf cos ime not.

The lars thing I want to say candud an between frends is that you musent git thinkin us bloks wot lives in the bush never gits no noos of anythink less than 6 munce old.

we opes to be able to pay yous a visit in town in a few weeks and ave a reel good yarn abowt rodes an crops an bush fires an bullicks an things. ime shure you will injoy our stay as we ingide yours if not moar.

we are orl rite ere ixcep things is very dry.

Yours truly
Ben Bowyang.

p.s. the missis wants to no wud you kinely inkwire the price of ½ doz ard warin servyets.

THE COOL CHANGE

FOR day on day an avid sun had drawn
Life-giving dews from leaf and frond and field;
Grey lay the grass upon the wilted lawn;
Gone half the garden's glorious floral yield.
No cloud was there to shield
Green things from those fierce rays that came with dawn
That Summer's flying, stinging pests might spawn.
Bees droned, cicadas reeled.

Now, suddenly, from out a northern hill
A savage wind tears all the forest thro',
Tossing and tugging at the trees until
The green mass seems to boil — a witch's brew
Not for a moment still.
Now the wind drops as sudden as it grew,
And all things wait, as if wise Nature knew
What next the gods should will.

Now, in the west, a black cloud lifts its head,
And, faint at first, a distant muttering breaks.
Chill and spasmodic little winds are sped
Down the still forest that once more awakes,
And all this green world takes
A saffron tinge. And, as the black clouds spread
Up to the zenith, comes a flash of red —
A crash — and all earth shakes.

Still gathered up, the turmoil holds aloof
A breath, then thunder crashes down the sky,
And, like some mighty herd on galloping hoof,
A far-off murmur waxes from a sigh
Into a wild, fierce cry
From tortured storm-wrack, like the weft and woof
Of God's great loom; and, drumming on the roof,
The deluge dashes by.

THE SONG OF THE SONGLESS SHEARER

"Back in the early days," said the old, grey shearer, "when we used the blades, and were all country men, and shearing was really shearing, we used to sing at the board the whole day through. But never a song is heard now. The shearers are mainly city men, who talk politics; and they are all keen on getting back to the city lights and the union meetings. We had better times in the days when we used to sing."

Now, my dad 'e was a shearer an' 'e sez to me, "Look 'ere.
There's sheep upon the run, me son; there's sheep we *'ave* to shear."
My dad 'e *was* a shearer, an' a country man as well.
'E sez to me, "If they ain't shore the country goes to 'ell."

My dad 'e *was* a country man (I think I told you that).
A man who knoo Australia where the sky-line's pretty flat.
'E never looked for spires an' things for cuttin' out the sky,
'E 'ad no vain desires an' things, the same as you an' I.

My dad 'e took the broader view, an' shore with dinkum shears,
An', oh, good Lord! down at the board — if any man 'ad ears —
'E'd 'ear 'em singin', singin' there while they ripped off the fleece.
An' me? Well I'm a shearer, but we've lorst them days o' peace.
For I lives down in the city; an' I knows the city's streets;
I 'ave to be on tap, yeh know, wot time the Union meets.

My father was a shearer, an' 'e knoo sheep thro' an' thro'.
'E never yearned for city lights, the same as me an' you.
My father was a country man; an' I am thinkin' now
My father picked the best of it — 'E sang things, any'ow.

An' when a man can't sing at work — sing shearin' at the board.
'E's losin' somethin' all the time that workmen can't afford.
Oh, me dad 'e *was* a shearer, an' 'e *was* a country man.
An' 'ere's me now, a shearer too; but sing I never can.

Fer why? I live in cities, an' the city's in me blood,
An' the Union boss 'as got me, an' — it's easy understud.
I goes to Union meetin's, an' they 'ands me all the dope.
But do I know Australia? No. I 'aven't got a 'ope.

I knows the cities an' the streets; an' when the shearin's due,
If you goes up or you stays down is wot the boss tells you.
Ah, me dad 'e *was* a shearer; an' 'e knoo sheep thro' an' thro'.
But I don't want to know 'em less they pay a man. Do you?

Yes; I'm a city shearer, an' when I get 'ome at night —
Back 'ome from these 'ere pitcher shows, an' p'raps a little tight.
I sorter gits to wonderin' if reely, after all,
My dad weren't on the dinkum track; an' ain't I took a fall —

Fer when me father shore a sheep 'e sung there at the board,
But shearers they ain't singin' now; for songs they can't afford.
They're thinkin' of the dough they'll get, an' 'ow they'll do it in.
But my dad sung to ringin' blades, an' never cared a pin.
An' this is all the change I get when all is done an' said:
If fellers cannot sing at work they might as well be dead.

TWO MEN

As I walked down a country road
  I passed two men upon the way.
High o'er the western skyline glowed
  The last gold coin of spendthrift day;
All thingss about me tribute paid
  To Autumn's bland munificence;
On fruits and corn the soft lights played,
  And flowers nodding by the fence.

As I walked down a country road
  I passed two men upon the track;
And one was bent beneath a load —
  His all, borne on an illclad back.
And one rode by in luxury
  Of cushioned ease and callous pride.
Yet I, who marked him well, could see
  That one unseen sat close beside.

As I walked down a country road
  I passed two men, and spoke them fair.
(O'er all things rich contentment flowed;
  For peace, and all God's gifts were there.)
One passed as if he had not heard;
  His eye held fear, his look was wild.
But, as I called a cheery word,
  The tattered man looked up, and smiled.

THE BROTHERHOOD OF EARTH

"For, notwithstanding every tribulation, the earth is a safeguard and . . . a security against ills of any kind. The earth remains when everything else has departed." — Passage from the will of a N.S.W. grazier, recently dead, who implored his sons to hold to the land.

WHILE we are of the earth is the earth our haven,
  The broad lands and the green grass under the sun.
Upon the heart of a man in this deep graven
  Whose toil is done
Out in the fields and the fallow lands and the stubble
  Where beasts are his brothers, and all things of earth
Stand to his need; in fair content, in trouble,
  The only worth.

We come of the clay and to the clay descending
  In its dark couch from all the upper strife
Find that deep peace that yet is not an ending,
  But unity of life
With the high stars and life past comprehension
  Of man's blunt senses born from out the sod.
Here is not burial, but an ascension
  To things of God.

Cleave to it then, my sons, that it may teach you
  The brotherhood of earth while earth things last,
That some foreknowledge, some dark hint may reach you
  Out of the vast
Unknowable that broods about those living
  Close to the soil and with the soil yet strive
That it may give them hope, and, in the giving,
  Keep faith alive.

Not from the skies above, not out of cities,
  Not thro' vague gropings of the human mind,
Not in the play of mortal hates or pities
  Such peace we find.
While we are of the earth shall earth uphold us,
  Our mother, teacher, and our one true friend
Till time and space be done, and joys enfold us
  With unity sans end.

FLOODBOUND
SOME BUSH PHILOSOPHY

UP here on the hill-tops, rain it ever so hard and long, the fears of flood is one anxiety that fails to touch us.

As Peter Parraday; the old-age pensioner, says: "This is the place from what the floods come; and it would be pretty tough for a man to get burned and drownded both."

So we keep our fears for the menace of the fire and, saving our sympathy for the unfortunate dwellers of the plains, suffer little from the depreda-tion of the waters.

Certainly we have our minor bothers. Swollen streams become unfordable for man and beast; all, or nearly all, of our hundred or more bridges, formed of chance-fallen trees, are well awash, and after such a deluge as this latest, hillsides become mere quaking blanc-mange-like masses from which great trees, losing their age-long root-hole, crash over roads; while washouts and minor landslides create temporary cascades and waterfalls, and from severed roots in roadside cuttings water gushes as from so many high-pressure water-pipes.

The most serious damage is to the cleared and cultivated hillsides. Here great gutters are graven in the plough and many yards of precious top-soil, with seed-potatoes, fertilizer and all, are washed into some swollen little creek and so carried to a river and the sea.

* * * *

IN this regard one is tempted to wonder how much of Victoria's precious fertile, life-giving earth, suspended in the yellow torrents pouring even now from many a river-mouth, has gone into the ocean.

On Saturday some of us journeyed down to inspect the vast inland sea that covers the Yarra flats; and the elder men, long resident there, said that never before had they seen such dark, earth-colored flood waters — "like pea-soup."

Certainly thousands, perhaps tens-, perhaps hundreds-of-thousands of acres, say four inches deep, have been filched from the State by the recent deluge — and the loss is irreparable.

It is the penalty of cultivation where cultivations is unwise— on wooded hillsides and forest lands where interlaced roots save many a washaway nature has her own wise way.

But, apart from very minor inundations of miniature river flats, our hilltop troubles have been light. As old Peter Parraday says, the waters of these steep-sided gullies rise up and talk a lot, but they don't lie down and sulk. Here they leave in haste to harry easier victims on the lowlands.

* * * *

STILL, we have had our little worries, and the records put up by this record down-pour have beaten even those of the most prolific Test match. I could never quote them all; but, for example, never before in man's memory has the creek risen as high as the old bullock track graven deep by the waggons of the first white man to reach this forest—fifty, sixty years ago.

Also, never before in history has Brogan's milking shed been entered by flood water. Though Pete Parraday says that ain't no good and proper reason for the tadpoles he found in his butter three days before the big rain began!

Which reminds me that our chief trouble concerns the same old Pete Parraday.

Late on Friday afternoon last a bushman arrived just in time to prevent the wilful old veteran from venturing upon a crazy footbridge over which at least four feet of flood waters flowed at the speed of an express train.

Forcible restraint had to be employed not so much because Pete's home was on the other side, but because his dog was— left there to guard the fowls.

* * * *

FINALLY, after half the settlement had gathered to argue with the obstinate dog-lover, it was seen that we were given three choices: Peter must be left to commit wilful suicide, or he must be forcibly imprisoned and guarded, or his dog must be brought over. Greatly daring, two young men, wading breast high, crossed on a fallen tree. But two hours' search failed to locate the dog.

So the young men waded back; and, as cold, weary and drenched from feet to neck, they passed George Jones's hut on this side, they discovered old Pete Parraday seated on the doorstep feeding his untroubled hound on tinned salmon. Nobody knows how that dog got across the creek, Pete says he jumped it—a mere matter of thirty feet or so.

Peter, by the way, has been with us on this side ever since. For the stout old veteran who on Friday would have faced almost certain death for the sake of a dog, has become a timid old man, fearing to venture, though the water over the footbridge is now only a matter of inches. Meantime, he has visited every house on this side more than once and always around mealtimes. He and his dog are waxing sleek, while hospitable housewives long for a final falling of the waters.

But, as old Pete says, what's a flood in these parts? Why in one or two months' time we shall probably be fighting bush fires.

BOWYANG'S BRIDGE

Meself an' ole Bill Smith this week,
We fell a gum tree 'cross the creek;
An ole man Bluegum, straight an' tall,
That shook Gunn's Gully with his fall.
We adzed 'er off all nice an' neat —
A real, fine ingineerin' feat,
An' fixed, for them as such require,
A hand-rail made of fencing wire.

Gunn's Gully's turnin' out today
To see me open 'er. An' say —
She is some bridge! An' don't forget
She ain't one penny piece in debt.
We tested 'er with Bill Smith's cow,
An' there she looms in beauty now,
Spannin' the creek, a monument
To proud Gunn's Gully's high content.

I 'eard from some bloke — dunno who —
They're openin' one in Sydney, too;
Some says a bigger one than this.
Aw well! two bridges ain't amiss,
An' if they get as much real joy
As me an' Bill from our new toy —
Good luck to them! The years will tell
If us an' them have built it well.

MOUNT TANGLEFOOT

ON Tanglefoot are found no stones
About the forest's leafy floor,
Save where a dead man's bleaching bones
Have lain these forty years, or more;
And there a cairn lifts, 'mid the trees,
Built patiently by grieving mates
To mark throughout the centuries
The sepulchre of old Bill Bates.

WHEN Tanglefoot lay deep in snow
Where paling-splitters had their shacks
The bullock teams were loth to go
Down to the plain o'er treacherous tracks;
But old Bill Bates, 'gainst all appeals,
Set out one morning with his load,
To fall beneath his waggon's wheels
And die upon the lonely road.

THEY found him when for long he'd lain
Half-hidden in a snowdrift there.
But paths were blocked now to the plain;
So, with a half-remembered pray'r,
They laid him in a shallow grave
Beside the track, his sorrowing mates.
"He was a white man," said Joe Shave —
The funeral rites of old Bill Bates.

THEN Jackson said to Peter Brent,
As the last clods above were prest:
"Ole Bill deserves a monument;
The wild dogs will not let him rest
Like this. I want, from every man —
Because Bill was a dead straight bloke —
A dinkum promise for my plan."
And solemnly the vow was spoke.

THEN day by day and week by week,
As slow teams sought the higher land,
A great stone from the foothill creek
Each bullocky bore in his hand;
And Peter Brent and Long Joe Shave
And Jackson and a dozen mates
Piled them all reverent on the grave
In memory of old Bill Bates.

ON Tanglefoot were once no stones
Where great trees yearn to rake the skies;
But now, above his bleaching bones,
A great cairn lifts where Bill Bates lies.
And as the teams plod up the hill
Men's hats are raised unto this day:
For men remember old Bates still,
Tho' all his mates are worlds away.

RESPITE

As we went down the ole bush road,
George Jones an' me the other day,
His bullicks tuggin' at their load,
We didn't have a lot to say;
But by the creek, George looks at me
Then sorter shakes his head in doubt.
"That ford is runnin' low," sez he.
"Looks like we're goin' to 'ave a drought."

Quick on that word my thoughts they flew
Back to a picture of the past:
The drought that came in ninety-two
Full half the countryside to blast.
I seen agen the dyin' stock,
The paddicks bare, the trees burned black;
I heard agen the evil flock
Of dark crows cawin' down the track.

I seen full plenty laid to waste
By arid wind and savage sun
Because mankind with sinful haste
Scatters earth's gifts as soon as won.
An' then I felt that sudden fear
That comes to men unsought, unguessed:
"If drought," I says, "comes to.us here
In this green place, what of the rest?"

But George, he cocks a weather eye
Above the trees. Sez he: "Take heart.
You ain't been noticin' the sky
I reckon somethin's due to start,"
Then sudden music sweet to hear,
Came singin' down the forest lane
To make an end to human fear,
It was the rain! The blessed rain!

THE ECONOMICS OF APPLECROP

GEORGE Alfred Applecrop guest-house proprietor and rustic philosopher, sat in a wheel-barrow on the shady side of the cow-shed, his head pillowed on sacking, and slept peacefully.

Around the corner of the shed came his friend and neighbor, Mr Theodore Budd, to waken him with loud words.

Save that his eyes opened and his lips moved in speech, George Alfred made no move.

"Shut up, can't yeh," said he. "Want to advertise a man to the listenin' world? Here I been trine to snatch a few winks, with me bad back an' everythink, an' if it ain't the roosters it's the poddies, an' if it ain't the poddies it's you, startlin' a man out of his hard-earned nap yellin' fool questions in his ear.

"Yes; 'hard-earned nap,' I said. When do you think the manager an' head an' front an' brains of a high class bush boardin' house gets time to think an' plan for the measly bit of profit that the city tourist leaves him? Every night an' all night I lays awake in the dark, when things is middlin' quite, excep' for the mopokes an' muskeeters, an' thinks out schemes.

* * * *

"Then, in the daytime, when I'm fair droppin' with fatigue an' me bad back an' everythink, I'm expected to sit out there in the sun in the paddick an' stop thecows from gettin' into the maize an' spuds.

"My wife, Em'ly's a good hard worker; but she ain't no manager. Many's an' many's the time I've laid awake beside her in the dark an' listened to her steady breathin' an' thought how lucky she was to be able to git tired enough to sleep all night.

"What's that? No! I ain't goin' to no Towrist Club meetin' this afternoon. In the first place, me back's too bad. Second, I got no time; I'm busy. An' third, the Towrist Club gives me a bad pain in the neck, an' I'm goin' to resign.

"Pretty lot of local boardin' house keepers they are: movin' an' secondin' an' carryin' idjiotic motions that is just spitin' their own faces an' takin' the profits outer the districts. Want to cut towrist tracks through the bush, do they. Nice lot of ec- conomists, I don't think. Stan's to reason. Towrist tracks is for towrists to walk on, ain't they. Well, a walkin' towrist is a hungry towrist; an' a hungry towrist eat's up your profits. An' the Towrist Club is goin' to cut towrist tracks an' give towrists appetites, are they? Not with my money they ain't. They gets no sub outer me this year. Why, I'd—

"Hey, listen! Was that Em'ly callin'?

"Just take a quick squint around that corner, will yeh; an' see if them cows has got into the spuds. They ain't? Goodo.

* * * *

"No; that ain't no one watchin' 'em. That's the scarecrow I shifted out of the orchard an' dressed in some of my own duds. At nights I hides him in the scrub. Awful like me in the distance, ain't he. More brain work. It's a bit of luck my wife, Em'ly's a wee trifle short sighted.

"What was we talkin' about? Oh, towrists. Yes; they got other bad faults besides appetites — these here new-fangled duds, f'rinstance. Gives a man's family notions. What with the girls wantin slacks an' shorts an' strides, an' the boys pesterin' me to buy 'em blazers and sweaters an' white flannin pants, a man don't get no peace. Born an' bred a four-piece man, I was; I been a four-piece man all me life—hat, shirt, pants, boots. That's all nature intended; an' anything else is just a bit of swank.

"Well, I can't waste time listenin' to you all day. You git to yer Towrist Club; an' you can tell 'em what I think of their economics.

"An', look. Would you do me the favor of walkin' round by that scarecrow an' talkin' to him for a few minutes so Em'ly can see you? Wave yer arms a bit to make it look natural. Thanks, Budd. So long."

And, two minutes later, George Alfred Applecrop, diplomat and economist, slept again in his barrow.

THE LAST SUNDOWNER

HE sat upon a fallen log
And heaved a long, deep sigh.
His gnarled hand fondling his old dog
As his gaze went to the sky.
"There goes another plane," said he —
"A soarin', roarin' pest!"
They robs a man of privacy,
An' motor cars of rest.

"Sundownin' ain't the game ut was
Since men have took to wings;
An' life grows narrer, jist because
Of planes an' cars an' things,
For the planes have pinched me privit skies
An' the cars have grabbed me earth.
An' all the news by wireless flies;
So what's sundownin' worth?

"Time was when I could sit me down
Where man had left no sign,
An' earth an' sky for miles aroun'
For that one hour was mine.
And I could sit an' think me thorts
An' watch the sun go west
Without no crazy ingine's snorts
To break into me rest.

"And as the afternoon grew late
I'd seek the haunts of men.
An' at some lonely homestead gate
I'd have sure welcome then;
An' tucker-bags were gladly filled,
And rest found for my back,
In change for bits of news I spilled
And gossip of the track.

"But now that wireless spreads its lies
From this and other lands,
They look on me with hard, cold eyes
An' give with grudgin' hands.
It's them that has to give me news;
And when I seek some wide,
Once silent scene, planes spoil me views,
An' cars honk me aside."

He sat upon a fallen log
And heaved a long, deep sigh.
"We're agein', me an' my ole dog,
An' old things have to die.
Sundownin's dead: men's minds an' ways
Is changin' with a jerk.
Seems like I'll have to end me days.
Travellin', in search of work."

TALL TIMBER

According to recent news, a snake which fastened on a man's leg at Burnie, Tasmania, was much disgusted upon finding that the leg was a wooden one.

THAT sort o' reminds me of ole days (said Bill)
In the bush at Toolangi, at Switherton's mill —
A sor-mill, you know — an' the sawyer we 'ad
Was ole 'Oppy McClintock, a wooden-legged lad.
'E was walkin' one day for to tighten a peg,
When a tiger snake grabs at 'is ole timber leg;
An' there it 'angs on, till I fetched it a crack,
But ole 'Oppy jist grins as 'e starts to walk back.

An' then somethink 'appens. We seen 'Oppy stop,
As 'e stumbles a bit, an' looks down at 'is prop
With a dead funny look. Then 'e lets out a yell:
"Ere, boys! Take it off me! It's startin' to swell!"
Well, we unstraps 'is leg, an' it swole an' it swole.
Snake pisen? Too right! 'Twas a twenty-foot pole.
In less than five minutes! Believe me or not.
An' as thick — It's as true as I stand on this spot!

We was 'eavin it out, when the boss starts to roar:
"'Ere! Why waste good wood? Shove it on to the sor!"
So we sors it in two, down the middle, an' then,
Them there slabs swole an' swole; so we sors 'em agen.
An' we sors, an' we sors; an' it swole, an' it swole
Till the end of the day, when the tally, all tole,
Was two thousan' foot super. You doubt it? (said Bill)
You ask any ole 'and up at Switherton's mill!

A BUSH CHRISTMAS

THE sun burns hotly thro' the gums
As down the road old Rogan comes—
The hatter from the lonely hut
Beside the track to Woollybutt,
He likes to spend his Christmas with us here.
He says a man gets sort of strange
Livin' alone without a change.
Gets sort of settled in his way;
And so he comes each Christmas Day
To share our bite of tucker and a beer.

Dad and the boys have nought to do,
Except a stray odd job or two.
Along the fence or in the yard.
"It ain't a day for workin' hard."
Says Dad: "One day a year don't matter much."
And then, dishevelled, hot and red,
Mum thro' the doorway puts her head
And says, "This Christmas cooking! My!
The sun's near fit for cookin' by."
Upon her word she never did see such.
"Your fault," says Dad. "You know it is.
Plum puddin'! On a day like this,
An' roasted turkeys! Spare me days!
I can't get over women's ways.
In climates sich as this the thing's all wrong.
A bit of cold corn-beef an' bread
Would do us very well instead."
Then Rogan says, "You're right; it's hot.
It makes a feller drink a lot."
And dad gets up and says, "Well, come along."

The dinner's served—full bite and sup.
"Come on," says Mum, "Now all sit up."
The meal takes on a festive air;
And even father eats his share
And passes up his plate to have some more.
He laughs and says it's Christmas time,
"That's cookin', Mum. The stuffin's prime."
But Rogan pauses once to praise,
Then eats as tho' he'd starved for days.
And pitches turkey bones outside the door.

The sun burns hotly thro' the gums,
The chirping of the locusts comes
Across the paddocks parched and grey.
"Whew!" wheezes Father. "What a day!"
And sheds his vest. For coats no man had need.
Then Rogan shoves his plate aside
And sighs, as sated men have sighed.
At many boards in many climes
On many other Christmas times.
"By gum!" he says, "That was a slap-up feed!"

Then, with his black pipe well alight,
Old Rogan brings the kids delight
By telling o'er again his yarns
Of Christmas tide 'mid English barns
When he was, long ago, a farmer's boy.
His old eyes glisten as he sees
Half glimpses of old memories,
Of whitened fields and winter snows,
And yuletide logs and mistletoes,
And all that half-forgotten, hallowed joy.

The children listen, mouths agape,
And see a land with no escape
From biting cold and snow and frost—
A land to all earth's brightness lost,
A strange and freakish
Christmas land to them.
But Rogan, with his dim old eyes
Grown far away and strangely wise
Talks on; and pauses but to ask
"Ain't there a drop more in that cask?"
And father nods; but Mother says "Ahem!"

The sun slants redly thro' the gums
As quietly the evening comes,
And Rogan gets his old grey mare,
That matches well his own grey hair,
And rides away into the setting sun.
"Ah, well," says Dad, "I got to say
I never spent a lazier day.
We ought to get that top fence wired."
"My!" sighs poor Mum. "But I am tired!
An' all that washing up still to be done."

THE SPORTING LIFE

BEN BOWYANG ENGAGED FOR THE TEST MATCH

gunns gully
march 5 1929

to the editor

deer sir

it is sum time now since i ave rote you an may be you an uthers as bin a bit put out over my deep an misteerius silens.

but as me an the uther primmer donners is in the abit of puttin it i want to ashure my deer publick that they ave never bin out of me thorts for wun minit.

i ave ad certin reesins for not ritin to you wich i ave refraned from maikin nown for feer of internashnil complecashuns an sevrin the crimsin bonds of kinship betwix ourselves and deer ole england

fack of the matter is i ave been so anoid over the barrakin i got abowt my previus letters to you that i ave been layin down

wen ever peeple ave started barrackin me i ave allus follered the best tradishins of the british empire an lade down

becos the modrin answer to the ole queschin stans england where she did is now no she layin down becos sumwun spoke narsty

but seein i ave bin layin down now for sevril munce without gittin anny reackshins an nobody taikin no notis i aint gittin much fun out of it

so i now taik up me pen to rite these few lines an make a siggistion to you wich i no will meet with grate aplause in yure offis

now it seams to me that these ere crikit squabils is gittin so seryus that thay looks like developin into sumpthink cachin if they aint nipped in the bud while the ine is ot

so wot i sez is let the erild ingage a just an imparshal man

to report the nex test match wich begins a fridy

wot you want is a man wot reely nos the gaim an wot aint one eyed an as got the curridge an the staminer to put them englishmen in ther proper place

altho i am pritty bizzy at present diggin me pertaters i am willin to cum down for me bare expenses an a small onerorium but not to small

you onley go to say the wurd

if you appen to be so fussy as to want evidens as to me boney fideys as a ixperk in criket i ave only got to pint out that i been umpirin the lokil matches ere for going on 3 seesins an doorin that time gunns gully aint lost a match

i ope you will agree to my siggestion abowt cumin down becos i think the fare way of reportin is the onley way if you want to preserve the good naim of crikit

my oan persnil opinyun is that crikit matches adent ort to be plaid at all becos thay is becomin to dangrous to them preshus silkin bonds wot is bindin us to the muther country

meself i agree intirely with mr jack ellis that crikit ad ort to be desided by arbitrashin

then the english teem needent leeve ome at all

they cud just lay down comfertable at ome an send out the evidens by wireless, for a imparshal juge to deside

instid of wich they are now onley gittin fleet streets nerves in ege to the pint of isteriks an playin duks and drakes with a nobul gaim—speshully duks

let me no irgint if you can afford to ingage me

i am sorry to ear mr chapman as got the flu

hoppin you are the saim

yures truly

Ben Bowyang

(Mr Bowyang has been engaged, and will reach Melbourne tomorrow—Ed.)

BOWYANG'S SELECTION

Harry Fungus for the Test

gunns gully
march 6 1929

the editor
the erild

deer sir

no dout you ave erd the sayin that fools rush in were anjils feer to tred

well i rekin i was a bit of a fool yestidy but ime a anjil today

wen you shode yure usal good jugement an grasped egerly at my offer to cum down to melbin an report the test match for you i was like a dawg with to (2) tin tales for the space abowt haf (½) a our

then wen i begun to relize wot terribul responsibilitys i ave tuk on i begun to git cole feet

wen i relize that i onley got to maik one (1) littel slip to ave the ole of the english press jumpin on me neck not to menshin the wiregrass watchman the gunns gully gazet the sidney sun an the rest of the privinshil press wen i relize that i go all goos flesh an feel like callin it off

but the blud of the bowyangs is thickern water and i aint never set me and to the plow yet an let it it me in the ribs

so if its me larst ack on this erth an i go down in the welter of gor still proclaimin that a good fast bowler is wurth more than rubys even if e does cut up the pitch ime goin to talk me life in me and an go down to that test match an tell the trooth

its goin to be ard orful ard and i relize that me poperlarity is goin ter git a terribul jolt but the trooth must prevale tho umpires fall

i never thot this criket was sich a serius bizness till i cum to reed abowt it in the papers lately and now ide sooner taik on mr bruces job or even be a juge of the arbitrashin cort rather than taik a chance as a criket experk.

* * * *

owsumever ime gaim an i got sumpthink to say right away that is proberly goin to git me into ot water an that is that we aint doin rite by our fast bowlers

wot is our selectors doin

are they serchin all over the country for the men we want

they aint

alexander was rite under ther noses an they never seen im till the dawgs begun to bark abowt im

but wot abowt the underds and underds of fast demin bowlers we got in the country ave the silectors ever seen em in axshun

they aint

why we got a fast bowler in gunns gullys unbeeten teem yung arry fungis wot cant be plaid in anny game with wooden stumps e is so fast e brakes em to splinters an we got to ave wikits maid outer bit of three quater ¾ pipin an even those gits bent dubble

but as the silectors ever seen arry fungis play or considered im for a test match to mo down the flour of england

they aint

wot i sez is that it is a skandal an a shaim

hoppin you are the saim

yures truly

Ben Bowyang

p.s. I will be down on the ground brite an erly a fridy mornin thanks for the tikits

BOWYANG'S TEST

He Begins His Duties

melbin crikit groun
7 am fridy

deer sir

i arriv in melbin lars nite as per contrack in good elth an spirits an fare stranin at the leesch to git me jurnalistic jootys of reportin this test match in my own fathful an original stile

as akordin to our agreement i am doin this job on time wurk an not peace work or per artikle i was down at the criket groun brite an early this mornin

but you are orful late risers here in melbin

you mitent beleeve it but altho the sun was well up there wasent a sole abowt

owever i am countin it in as time on jooty as it wernt my falt ther was nuthink doin

so i went back to the pub an had a bit of brekfus then i cum back an as there was still no wun abowt i clum over the fence so as to be sure of a seet

8.20 a.m.

you mitent bleeve it but been chuked out an ime ritin his gen. a tree in the moter park an i rekin ime ernin me muney

9.5 a.m. fridy

i ave clum over the fence agen an tore wun (1) pare of pants for wich i will charge on my akount

this jurnlistick life as its ups and downs asnt it

the gaits is now open and to (2) men ave cum in but thay aint startid playin yet

11.20 a.m.

i been avin a bit of a nap avin slep poorly lars nite

there is a orful lot of peepil ere but you is terribul slow startin yure matches in melbin

11.45 a.m.

england as won the toss

sumow i dont think this is goin to be mutch of a match

12 miday

thay is cumin out

12.30 p.m.

ime orful sorry but i bin too ixcited to rite anythink for the last arf (½) our

the skore now is jardeen 12 obbs 5 extrees 3 totil 10

ime orful ixcited

gosh that wun neerly got im

why dont they chuk in quicker
jardeens cot out
no e aint
wot sort of umpirin do thay cal that
the man sittin nex me will git wot es lookin for if he dont stop chipin the orstralians
orray obbs is stumped
no e aint
the umpirins rotten
the skores is
neerly cot neerly cot ows that umpire
the skore is
this is the slowest battin i ever see

12.50 p.m.

if its all the saim to you mister editer ile leeve the rest of my ritin til i git back to the pub tonite an git a bit of peese

ime that ixcited now i dunno wether ime on me ed or me eels

hoppin you are the saim

yures truly
Ben Bowyang

ps 1.40 p.m. jardeen is run out
ps no 2.15 p.m. the umpire sez e aint this is orful

BEN AT THE TEST

Faster at Gunn's Gully

melbin
fridy nite

deer sir

wel i ave saw a test

i no yure reeders will ixcuse me for not ritin more abowt it yestidy but i was orful ixcited for the first half(½) our becos i was lookin forward to sumpthink reel thrillin it been me furst test

but only for the furst arf our

after that the more i looked forward the more i giv up ope of never seein nuthink after the first arf our wen me glad opes for sum innercent fun begun to drupe an dy i cud ave rit you ten (10) leedin artikles six (6) colums of gardnin notes an sevril luv letters an then ad time over to ponder on the mistrys of umin life an the swift an terribul energy of a gaim of drafts betwix bil smith an jim airey on bills back vranda on a hot sundy afternoon an long for ome an the wild gaety of the ectick bush

wots rong with me as i aint unerstud wot cricit reely is

up at gunns gully we got a ole fashioned ideer its a gaim

Crickit aint a gaim its a solem rite

if they had a put them flags arf marst yestidy an sumone ad struck up the ded march in sorl i wud a stood up an bowed me ed reverint an sed a prare for the corps

after this i aint blamin the barakers anny more for yellin and goin on

Thay got to yell to keep one anuther awake

wots the matter with me is i got the rong ideer of crickit altogether

it aint the crikiters wot makes crikit its the crowd

its wot thay calls mob sikology

jist eemagin to yerself if you ad the melbin crickit groun all to yerself an was sittin ther aloan watchin jardeen maik ninteen (19) runs in a hundrd (100) an wun (1) minits wud you sooner go on sittin or go over to the botanik gardins and watch the tempetchus snales gallopin madly over the orticulcher

ide git reel giddy lookin at snales after a our of mr jardeen shuvin a slab of timber in frunt of a lether stone

mind you i aint sayin nuthink agen crikit or agen mr jardeen an is feller stachers

the trubble is i got the rong ideer of crickit

up in gunns gully we got to taik a rest cure AFTER a cricket match

but the uther methid as its pints if you ad a late nite or sore feet

owever i was orful glad to see obbs maik is underd an i foun meself cheerin im with the rest

that lad has the cut of a reel good bushman an ide like to see im swingin a ax

anyways ime lernin an i picked up a fey pints yestidy from the uther fellers in the stand

tomorrer ime going down with a book an a cushin an sumpthink in a bottil

them blokes nos ow to injoy a reel crikit match an ime lernin

i spose you seen the scores in the paper but if you dident it dont matter.

i mite ave sumpthink ixcitin to tell you tomorrer

in the meantime i still remane opeful but orful sore

hopin you are the saim

Yures truly

Ben Bowyang

ps that scorers got a orful soft job aint e

BEN FINDS EXCUSES

Why Batting is Slow

melbin

march 12

deer sir

i no wots the matter with me now

i aint got the test match temperment

all thru the furst cupler days i been bored to teers with the slow skorin of the inglishmen i been tellin meself that as soon as the ossies got in we was goin to see fire wurks

i been tellin meself that these ere efeet inglish plairs altho thay is verry nice fellers aint got the dash an viger an the staminer of our fellers

so i rote to bil smith up at gunns gully and i sez jist you wate i sez jist you wate till our men gits to the wikits an then yule see sum reel crikit like you gits at gunns gully sumpthink with a bit of ackshin in it you wate

wel the ossies is at the wikit all rite but i dunno

i wated all day yestidy

i ad a good seet an i wated an i went on watin

but i never seen nuthink that gimme the erge to send up a grate shout to the igh valts of even

i never seen nuthink that maid me want to tork abuv a wisper

wich was praps jist as wel becos if i ad sed it abov a wisper the pleece mite ave erd me

but mind you i aint sayin nuthink agen the ossies

i aint no carpin critik mind you thay done wot they done becos it ad to be done

i agree with all the uther experks that while the inglishmen was orful dull an tame an dedly monotinus wen thay was skorin so slow the ossies was reely playin brillyunt crickit wen thay done sackly the saim thing

you see it was the saim thing onley it was diffrunt

it was altogether diffrunt

an it was diffrunt becos in a manner of speekin—

i mean if you look at it the rite way

well wots the good of torkin

you ask anny of the uther experks an thay will tell you

ask anny of the crowd wot was there an thay will tell you the ossies batted slow becos thay ad to bat slow agen sich bowlin an it aint a bit of use arguin becos i no

an anny man wot sez diffrunt can cum an ave it out with me

i dunno wot ime gittin all otted up abowt but wen i ear a man wot dont no nuthink about the gaim sayin that the ossies is a lot slower than the inglishmen wy i—i

o well i dunno ave it yer oan way

ave it anny way you like

annyways ime goin down agen today to do a bit more watin

but i find watin orful ard becos as i say i aint got the reel test match temperment

a test match temperment is the saim temperment wot ole jim airey as got

ten yeer ago e tuk out a inshurince policy agen being struk by litenin an e is still livin in opes

torkin of opes wy dont sum wun tell yung jackson to put spikes in is boots

fancy losin a match for the sake of a spike its enuf to make the ole crowd spikey

hoppin you are the saim,

yures truly

Ben Bowyang

BEN REVEALS SECRET MISSION

Bradman for Gunn's Gully

melbin

march 13

deer sir

now wot abowt the ossies

aint i sed all along wot was goin to appin an aint it cum tru

as a crikit experk i rekin i stand aloan

but wile i was down there at the ground yesterdy i neerly fergot to behave like the perfeck test match habituay wot i ave lerned to becum

besides me cushin an me lunch bag an me bottil i ave now lerned to take along a pare of oprey glasses an a bored look

but i neerly fergot meself yesterdy an let a yell outer me wen bradman startid nockin em abowt

i think the bloke nex me muster thort i ad the ikkups

i think praps instid of givin me a tikit for the stand in fucher you mite git me a pass for the outer were i mite find more room fer self ixpreshun

but i am ramlin on like this becos reely i got a confeshin to maik to you an i dunno ow to begin

fack o the matter is i ad to (2) strings to me bo wen i cum down ere to report this test match for you an i been drorin dubble exes but that is neether ere nor there an not wurth discussin

but wot i do wish to announce is that i been actin ere as speshil comishner for the gunns gully crikit club an have been in constant comunicashin with ther secatry mr bil smith with a vew to gettin old of likely players for the club

littel did the orstralian batsmen think as thay went out to the wikits that the egil ey of a silector was watchin evry move but i never let it be nown befor for feer it mite make them nervis owever i ave now maid up my mind an i can let the cat outer the bag

* * * *

las nite i wired bil smith urgint as follers

ave found the rite man for our club good stile ard itter but keeps em a bit to low for long grass an ferns will i ingage im ben bowyang

an this mornin i receeved the follerin from bil

ingage im can git im job on rode wurk comitey unanimus excep arry fungis oo is jelis can git im bord an login my place oo is e bil smith

so it is now my pleesin jooty to announce that the gunns gully crikit club preemiers unbeeten for thre (3) seesins runnin with my umpirin now offers a place in its teem to this yung bradman an we can give im a stidy job on the noo rode an good tuker at bils place

it is a oner that praps e dident look for but the gunns gully silecters is very diffrunt frum yures down ere an alwiz beleeves in ingagin yung blud before it gits ardnin of the artries

of corse bradman will ave to learn a few noo rules befor e plays in our teem sich as not out wencot off of trees and thre (3) runs for ball lost in braken an cetra but thats eesy

ime goin down agen brite an erly today to run me ey finly over this yung plaier an will then maik im a formil offer in my ofishal capasity

or i mite put it off for a day or to (2) so i can keep on drorin them dubble exes

i ope to see sum good play today an more continyus as them inglishmen mitent be so orful thursty

hoppin you are the saim

yures truly

Ben Bowyang

BOWYANG'S DEFENCE

Trouble With Gunns Gully

melbin, march 14

deer sir

i dunno but ime gittin in all of a tangel over this test match

ere the gunns gully club as impowred me to ingage this yung bradman an e goes an gits isself out yesterdy befor i ad ime to git downto the ground yesterdy an run afinal ey over im

and now i dunno

grimmit an ornybrook sorter took me fancy yesterdy an then the way that there oldfield got isself into to (2) places at wunce an cot jardeen out wile keepin wikits an feeldin at squar leg verry neerly got im into the gully teem on the spot

but i cant taik em all becos ther aint enuf jobs up there to go round an the lokal blokes on the rode job is neerly all in the teem an cant be sacked

annyways i think ile leeve it till the end of the test to maik me choice

so i am wirin bil smith ackordin

i got a snaiky letter frum bil yestidy sayin ow the teem cant stand payin my exes if this test lasts mutch longer

bil sez its awl rite listnin in but as ther aint anny work gittin done they mite as wel awl be down ere lookin on as up there listnin in

bil sez i got awl the thick end of the stick an me reports of the match is rottin annyway but thats is jelisy

bil sez if the test lasts to (2) or thre (3) more weeks i ad a rite to cum ome an give sum wun else a chanct

* * * *

bil sez as ow ime a low down skeemer annyow wot is drorin exes frum the teem under fals pertences

wich is pritty ot seein as ow as presidint an umpire of the club i giv em a arf ginee donashin thre (3) yeer ago an ave promised em anuther as soon as the rode bord gives me a metil rode to cart me spuds

some peepil aint got no sens of gratichood

owever i ave replide dignifide pointin out that if uthers ad the gift of ritin that i ave thay wud be ere in my place an my jurnlistick jootys pervents me leavin melbin at this jungcher wich i sined i ave the oner to be yures an cetra to maik it formil an bindin

a man aint annywere in this wurld if e dont stick up for is rites

i am sorry to introod these privit matters in yure paper but i beleeve in bein open an above bord an sum things need publicity

an now i aint got space to say mutch abowt yesterdys play but i ave no doubt all as been sed wot can be sed an if it aint sed sum wun will say it since i been down ere it seams to me that were crikit is kinserned there aint mutch left unsed

not even by the barakers

listnin to sum of em yestidy maid me fare ashamed of me nativ land

if we ad that sort up at gunns gully thay wudent make nun of them remarks twice

we may be ruf but we are respectibil

hoppin you are the saim

yures truly

Ben Bowyang

"PUT ON BEN BOWYANG!"

Difficulties Explained

Melbin
March 15

deer sir

befor i say annythink els i want to maik a persnil explanashin

down at the test match yestidy a porshin of the crowd wen the inglishmen was nokin the bowlin abowt a bit begun to yel out put on Ben Bowyang

at first i could ardly beleeve me oan eers

but thay was yellin for me awl rite an i begun to sispect a bit of sarkasm and thort sumwun was trine to chuck orf

but wen i see mr rider cast a angshus look were i was sittin i seamed to deteck a note of sinserity in the crowds demand

put on ben bowyang thay sez sort of desprit

so i think a persnil explanashin is joo to the publik

in the furst plaice i aint a credited member of the orstralian teem an secindly i got an ideer me bowlin days is over

no dout the crowd must ave erd sum way abowt me grate feets of bowlin up at gunns gully back in the old days wen i got a dubble at trick with the elp of a poly cow wot ad walked over the pitch in wet wether the nite befor

i ave no dout also that the crowd wud ave been delited if i ad gon out an skittiled mr tates stumps but me jints aint so suppel as they was an i ave lost the nack of brakin to (2) foot frum the laig side like i used to

owever i wish to thank them as called on me and ope this xplanashun will serv

wel we ad a grate days crikit yestidy

the way them inglishmen got mode down reminded me of our good ole gunns gully matches

it out or git out thats our stile

i got to admit that me art was in me mouth a cupler times wen mr rider missed them to (2) catches but the leest sed abowt that the better

a man dosent want to go comitin lesee magesty an git unpopler

the onley way i can akount for im missin em is that the air must ave bin a bit bumpy yestidy

praps the ball struck a air pokit jist befor it got to im i cant think of annythink else an still keep me ally good in collinwood

annyway we ar goin to ave a grate day today an if the ostralian teem dont win ans down ime goin to ishoo a formal chalinge for them to cum up an play the gully teem

wich remines me that i ave jist erd about this country crikit weak in melbin an you mite be amazed to no that no wun wurd as been sed abowt bringin down our teem

thay cant maik it out a oversite becos i ave now maid the teem well nown an the onley thing that can akount for it is eether jelisy or feer

jist becos we dont play this ere parler crikit wot is onley fit for a yung ladys bordin skool but is reely e men crikiters an a bit ruf in our methids our claims as been ignored by them runnin the country weak

awl i can say is that if thay are afrade of us why aint they manly an upright enuf to admit it

i am now goin down to the ground to git a good seet an yell me ed orf in spite of the nice ole gents in the members stand

but if we lose its goin to be orful tuf becos gunns gully wont ingage anny men out of a beeten teem

we got our pride an as the champeen teem of the districk we aint taikin no risks with men wot as proved themselfs dismil failyers

hoppin you are the saim
yures truly
Ben Bowyang

BEN FINDS IT DULL

Why Cricketers Should Start Young

melbun
march 16

deer sir

wel i was down at the crikit ground agen yestidy avin a look at the statchery

now and then i seen sum of em move an it was very interestin

if the orstrailans is goin to win this match why dont thay git it over an dun with an put thurty thousan peepil out of ther aginy

wot this match is developin into is shear croolty to crikit fans

ime a active man meself an i ave led a strenyus life an ere i been doin nuthink for a ole week but sit down an put on wate

i rekin i must ave gained arf a stone since larst friday weak

an i want to apolagise to mr jardeen for wot i sed about is slow skorin the uther day

compared with sum uthers i cud menshin mr jardeen is a wirlin urrican

ime orful sorry to ave to say it but I rekin the noospapers is responsible for this slow skorin

its these ere press fotografers

the crikiters as got so used to avin there foters tuk so often thay are alwiz posin for em in case sum wun mite want to taik a snap

anny way i no now why thay call them test matches

so far as i can see the publick is goin to win this test

but if it lasts till the publick pashens is wore out and thay stop goin to the ground then it will count as a win for the crikiters

this letter mite seam to you sorter grumlin an grouchy but mine you i aint chukin orf at yure crikit down ere it as its brite spots and is orl rite as far as it goes wen it does go

but you gotter remember this is the second saterdy i ave missed the match up at gunns gully an wen i think of em up there this afternoon tarin orl over the lanscape turnin ansprings over logs an nocken sixers into the skrub every to (2) minits you cant blaim a man for gittin omesick for a bit of ackshin

besides thay got a noo umpire in my place an that mite meen them losing a match

owever ime goin down to the match today an if i see anythink movin i will wire you urgint

i will rite you a sumry of me ideers an final opinyuns on mundy and then me for ome an a bit of reel excitemint watchin me spuds growin

praps ime gittin to old for crikit

crikit is a yung mans gaim after all an the orstralians is wise to put these colts in the teem

thay is then abel to play out a match before ole age overcums em and ther jints begin to creek

well ime hoppin for the best today altho the wether looks dull

hoppin you are the saim

yures truly

BEN BOWYANG

p.s. from the ground

kipax is ran out

that just shows you the danger of movin in this gaim

BEN SAYS GOODBYE

Debacle at Gunns Gully

melbin
march 18

deer sir

wel orstralia as wun the injurince test

i ad ideers wen i cum down ere to report this match for you that if the ossies wun i was goin to be to ixcited to old me pen an rite abowt it

i oan i was ixcited down there on saterdy wen that grate scorer mr bye got a forer an wun the match for us

but today i ave ad a orful nock back

i ave ad a shok to me sistem wot as robbed me of all the joy of the ossies victry

orstralier as won all rite but wot is fur more importint gunns gully as lost

for the fust time in thre (3) yeers my ole teem as been beet jist becos i wasent there umpirin in my oan just and imparshil manner

no less than six (6) of our men was giv out lbw by a underand skoundril wot is trine to curry favor with the captin of the uther side so as to git a stiddy job with the council

but wate til i git ome

thers goin to be a protest an if i aint maid ead serang an sole arbitrater akount of me ixperk nolege gained at this ere test there is goin to be sumpthink doin up at the gully

six out lbw

its perpostris

an yule agree with me that thers sumpthink crook wen i tell you that wun of them men as a woodin laig wot the bail appened to it

ow can a man be out lbw wen the laig aint there but is berrid up in is back paddick for goin on seventeen yeer

e tuk it ome from the orspitle an planted it there so as e cud say e was the onley man on erth wot looked after the flours on is own grave

an then thay goes an gives im out lbw for a laig that as been ded for seventeen yeer

jist wate til i git ome

* * * *

wel i aint in no mood to rite you a long letter

i was ixcited enuf on saterdy an i shud ave rit you then an sung me peens of joy on orstralias victry

i ung about the ground for to (2) ours after the match to trine see mr bradman abowt jinin up with the gunns gully teem but i neevr seen im

it was like lookin for a needil in a aystack

owever i will rite im persnil

today i am ketchin the trane for ome an i cant say ime sorry

i taik this operchunity to wish you an yure reeders manny appy returns of the day as it is an oliday and o revor

an i want to thank all them peepil wot as rit to me sayin

nice things abowt my jurnalistick wurk

it makes a man feel good to no is wurk is not in vane but wen i think of that gunns gully match i go all ot up the neck

hoppin you are the saim

yures truly

Ben Bowyang

BOWYANG AT HOME

Rustic Contentment

gunns gully
novemer 7th

to the editer of the herald

dere sir

as you will see by this letter i am ome agen an glad to be there

i ave never felt so bonzer in awl me life as i am feelin this Sundee afternoon sittin ere ritin this letter after a gloryus trip to the cup an awl me expensive otel bil paid by the nice kind bookmakers an presents for awl the fambly an a large wad left over to put in soke for a raney day

me an bil smith torked it over on saterdee nite after we cum back frum the racis where we was both reel lucky

at leest i wudent go so fur as to say lucky so mutch as branes becos bil followed my tips an we both backed rarin an gildry an pantheen an i finished up with over 130 pouns an bil ad neerly 60 to the good

i tell you it maid us reel nervis avin awl that munney abowt our close in the city my left and as still got the cramps where i been holdin on to that role of notes in me pockit

there was wun crook lookin bloke at our otel wot i ad me spishins abowt

e looked to me like wun of them confidence speelers an e seamed to keep follerin us about

i found out after that e was a rich squatter frum the westrin districk but a man cant be to carful in the city

so me an bil torked it over an bein well ahead of the gaim we maid up our mines to ire a privit moter car to taik us ome in stile at daylite sundee mornin

so thats wot we dun an i was glad we did becos i was to nervis to sleep awl nite thinkin i cud ear sumwun tryin our door an avin to keep feelin under me piller to see if we munney was safe

it was a grate trip

an ere i am of a bewtiful sundee afternoon full up to the neck of gentleness and piece

the missus as gon to church warin the swank fur thing an the noo at an boots an cetrer wot i bot er out of my winnins an she looked so orful toffy wen she ad em awl on i riz me at to er sort of unconshus

i rekin there is a lot of feemail arts avin spasms in gunns gully chapil today

me secund eldist boy clarens is out shootin rabbits with the noo amerliss gun i bot for im an i can ear im poppin evry five minits

the uther kids ave fixed up the noo wireliss gagits i bot em and this mornin thay awl went to church in melbun adlade sidney an brisbin avin a bit of the servis in ech city

bil smith bot imself a noo acorjin out of is winnins an i can ere im at is plaice up on the ill tryin art to play valencher as a him of prase for kind bookmakers

an outside the sun is shinin an the littel dicky burds is twitterin an the pigs is squeelin with delite an the whole Bowyang fambly is that pleezed with their selfs an the presents i bot em as a lot of dawgs with 2 tin tales apeace

an in the tee cady on the mantil peace is a nice littel role of 5 quid notes wot i ave got left over after the good bookeys ave bot awl these things an pade that otel bil wot kep me awake at nite an give me nervis dispepsy evry time i et

an just wile i been ritin this letter i ave jist rememered that i cleen fergot to by annythink for meself an i cud do reel well with a noo pipe an a pare of brasis

. but praps sum nice bloke mite win a wad sum day an give em to me

but the onlay uther bloke in gunns gully oo as wun on the racis besides me an bil is ole alf appilyard at the post office and e is to meen to give 3 cheers

hoppin you are the saim

yures truly

BEN BOWYANG

THE GAME

The football season opens today

IT'S many and many a long year now since first a fellow killed a cow and robbed the creature of its hide. Then, when he'd scraped the hairy side, he tanned it in a noisesome pit and made a little bag from it.

But, finding it would not hold air he wandered to a forest where there grew strange trees, and found that some contained a queer resilient gum. So, being quite a clever chap, he lined his leather bag with sap: then took a long, long breath and blew. Red in the face he puffed anew until the bag was blown up tight: a thing elusive, hard yet light, that to the slightest blow would yield. And then he flung it in a field.

A score of tribesmen gathered there beheld the object, light as air that bounced along, and, as it came: "A game!" they shouted. "Here's a game!"

One seized the thing and rushed away. (Man had discovered how to play.) He ran, he stumbled, almost fell, and after him there rushed, pell-mell (each seeking madly to secure and hold this strange elusive lure) the whole excited, yelling tribe.

'Tis hardly fitting to describe the scene that followed after that — the scene where men cursed, struggled, spat, bit, gouged, kicked, mauled and madly tore from other men the skins they wore. The scene of maimed men lying round in twos and threes upon the ground, the sight of spent men out of breath, of battle riot, sudden death.

But all agreed, when it was o'er, they'd never had such fun before, and all agreed it closed too soon — a very pleasant afternoon.

And yet if you go down today, and hear the yells and watch the play, you'll find the prehistoric game and modern football much the same. You'll notice your subconscious rise, responding to the savage cries, until the primal man once more, uprising as he did of yore, impels you to stand up and hoot, "Yah! Tear 'em down! Put in the boot!"

And, though you blush for what you've done, you can't deny it's lots of fun.

THE BARRACKER

Demonstrations by angry crowds against football umpires and individual players were made on three Melbourne grounds on Saturday.

LARGE mouth and little head,
Loud voice and idle brain,
Reason, judgment, caution shed.
"Pull 'im down! Yah! Crook again!"

A crook day Saturdee. Say, was you there?
I never seen a football match so tame.
The bloomin' umpire acted strickly fair!
Why, strike a light! You don't call that a game!
'E never done a thing to nark the crowd.
Them spoil-sports 'adn't ought to be allowed.

'Ow can a decent bloke injoy a match
Unless there's somethin' 'e can 'oot about?
A dead crook game. There wasn't one bright patch
Where we could tell 'im off or count 'im out.
'E done 'is best to please both sides. The coot!
We 'ad no chance of puttin' in the boot.

One-eyed and partisan,
Folly loose and fairness fled —
A sorry semblance of a man.
"Crack 'im! Yah! Knock off 'is 'ead!"

Gimme the days when umpires makes mistakes —
Somethin' to put some ginger in the game,
When reason's chucked aside an' passion wakes
An' 'owls run round the benches like a flame,
When blokes gits reel worked up an' yell fer blood
An' even ladies takes to chuckin' mud.

Give me the days with langwidge flowin' free,
'At-pins an' pickets an' a all-in fight
An' broken fences. That's the stuff for me.
It's better than the Stajim of a night.
A bloke's reel nacher then gits dinkum play.
But ideel umpires? Wot? Aw, fade away!

THE COMMENT IRONIC

According to the cabled report of the first English-South African test match at Birmingham, South Africa began their first innings to ironical comments from 11,000 spectators.

DID you say barracking? Oh, come! What, what?
Never in England, sir! It isn't done.
Do you suggest invective? Oh, what rot?
It must be just that cable fellow's fun.
"Comment ironic", yes, but never "skite".
One may be quite ironic yet polite.

For we never say Boo!
As Australians do
With a loud and vociferous bellow.
And vulgar abuse?
Oh, I say, what the deuce!
Would you take a rise out of a fellow?
I mean to say — What?
When our passions wax hot
We may even wax slightly satiric,
But not in the way
That Australians may
When the barracking lifts to the lyric.
I will even admit,
Should the circumstance fit,
We may even grow mildly sardonic;
And you'll hear in the hush
Some loud fellow cry "Tush!"
Well, that is a comment ironic.

But barracking! In Birmingham? Tut, tut!
The thing's unthinkable! There's not a doubt.
Faint murmuring may be indulged in; but
Should any person seek to rise and shout
Ill-bred expletives and that sort of rot,
Why, dash it all, the fellow would be shot!

Tho' Australians may,
I am sorry to say,
Grow exceedingly coarse in the outer;
And, in fashion quite crude,
Hurl their epithets rude
At a bowler, or batsman or scouter;
In Britain our style
Is to mark by a smile
Or a frown or some fleeting expression

Our views of the play
In a cultural way;
For we're devilish good at repression.
And if some grave breach
Should impel us to speech
It's mellifluous, mild and euphonic.
Should the play be quite bad
We may mutter "Egad!"
And that is a comment ironic.

DEFINITIONS

If Bradman continues as he has begun on English wickets there is a danger that he will lose all claim to the title of "batsman", not so much because of his unconventional methods, as because of the sheer lack of any means of comparison. He is in a class apart.

WE have heard it. Oft we heard it long before we came of age.
In whatever fields we practise, art whatever arts engage:
Ever praise for the performance, still begrudging utmost fame,
From who would extol the action yet withhold its hallowed name.
Thus, in painting, think how often, praise is mingled with complaint:
"No, of course the man's no 'artist' but, by jove, sir, he can paint!"

AS in fields of art and letters, tho' Australian pride has swelled
We may never match our betters while the title is withheld,
So in sport. Consider racing. This young champion. What a horse!
At all distances breaks records, old and new, on every course.
But the veterans, harking backward, ban the upstart with a word:
"Yes; no doubt the nag has speed, sir. But a 'racehorse'? Bah! Absurd!"

WHEN the Digger put a show up Over There — some push or road —
He won almost fulsome praise: "The bravest thing God ever made."
But it seemed he still lacked something — something vague and undefined
That would make him, if he had it, the supremest of his kind.
And 'twas said in all good feeling of the valiant Aussie band:
"These men never will make 'soldiers'. But as fighters? Gad, sir! Grand!"

THO' he skittled English wickets till their every hope grew bleak,
Ernie Jones was ne'er a "bowler". No, sir. Just a sort of freak.
There's a danger in perfection that may set a man apart;
What he gains in execution he may lose, 'twould seem, in art.
Now there's Bradman, freak run-getter, making scores till all is blue.
Can we call this man a "batsman". Speaking honestly, would you?

A POST-CUP TALE

I' ad the money in me 'and!
Fair dinkum! Right there, by the stand.
  I tole me wife at breakfus' time,
  Straight out: "Trivalve," I sez "is prime.
Trivalve," I sez. An', all the week,
I swear ther's no one 'eard me speak
  Another 'orse's name. Why, look,
  I 'ad the oil straight from a Book
On Sund'y at me cousin's place
When we was torkin' of the race.
  "Trivalve," 'e sez. "'Is chance is grand."
  I 'ad the money in me 'and!

Fair in me 'and I 'ad the dough!
An' then a man 'as got to go —
  Wot? Tough? Look, if I 'adn't met
  Jim Smith (I ain't forgave 'im yet)
'E takes an' grabs me be the coat.
"Trivalve?" 'e sez. "Ar, turn it up!
'Ow could 'e win a flamin' Cup?"
  Of course, I thort 'e muster knoo.
  'Im livin' near a trainer, too.

Right 'ere, like that, fair in me fist
I 'ad the notes! An' then I missed —
  Missed like a mug fair on the knock
Becos 'is maggin' done me block.
"That airy goat?" 'e sez. "E's crook!"
Fair knocked me back, 'e did. An' look,
  I 'ad the money in me 'and!
  Fair in me paw! An', un'erstand,
Sixes at least I coulder got —
Thirty to five, an' made a pot.
Today I mighter been reel rich —
  Rollin' in dough! Instid o' which,
'Ere's me — Aw! Don't it beat the band?
I 'AD THE MONEY IN ME 'AND!
  Put me clean off, that's wot 'e did . . .
  Say, could yeh len' us 'arf a quid?

HOW WE BACKED THE FAVORITE

"SURE thing," said the grocer; "as far as I know, sir,
  This horse, Peter Pan, is the safest of certs."
"I see by the paper," commended the draper,
  "He's tipped and he carries my whole weight of shirts."
The butcher said, "Well, now, it's easy to tell now
  There's nothing else in it except Peter Pan."
And so the baker, the barman, bookmaker,
  The old lady char and the saveloy man.

"You stick to my tip, man," admonished the grip-man,
  "Play up Peter Pan; he's a stayer with speed."
And the newspaper vendor, the ancient road mender,
  And even the cop at the corner agreed.
The barber said, "Win it? There's nothing else in it.
  I backed Peter Pan with the last that I had."
"Too right," said the liftman. "The horse is a gift, man."
  The old jobbing gardener said, "Peter Pan, lad!"

I know nought of racing. The task I was facing,
  It filled me with pain and unreasoning dread.
They all seemed so certain. And yet a dark curtain
  Of doubt dulled my mind . . . But I must keep my head!
I went to the races, and I watched all their faces.
  I saw Peter Pan's; there was little he lacked.
And as he seemed willing, I planked on my shilling
  And triumphed! And that's how the favorite was backed.

GALLOPING HORSES

OH, this is the week when no rhymster may rhyme
On the joy of the bush or the ills of the time,
Nor pour out his soul in delectable rhythm
Of women and wine and the lure they have with 'em,
Nor pen philosophic if foolish discourses,
Because of the fury of galloping horses.

Galloping, galloping thro' the refrain —
The lure and the lilt of it beat on the brain.
Strive as you may for Arcadian themes,
The silks and the saddles will weave thro' your dreams.
Surging, and urging the vision aside
For a lyrical lay of equestrian pride,
For the roar of the race and the call of the courses,
And galloping, galloping, galloping horses.

This is the week for the apotheosis
Of Horse in his glory, from tail to proboscis.
That curious quadruped, proud and aloof,
That holds all the land under thrall of his hoof.
All creeds and conditions, all factions and forces,
All, all must give way to the galloping horses.

Galloping, galloping — sinner and saint
March to the metre, releasing restraint.
If it isn't the Cup it's the Oaks or the Steeple
That wraps in its magic the minds of the people.
Whether they seek it for profit or pleasure,
They all, willy-nilly, must dance to the measure.
The mood of the moment in all men endorses
The glamorous game and the galloping horses —
Galloping horses — jockeys and courses —
They gallop, we gallop with galloping horses.

THE NARK

WAIT till after Chewsdy, wife.
'Taint far ahead to look,
A change is comin' in your life,
Or else I'm much mistook,
I'll buy you rugs an' furs an' things
An' di'monds by the ton.
We're 'ome at last when Chewsdy's past
An' Melbun Cup is run.

Wait till after Chewsdy, Bill.
You're silly if you frets;
I'll pay that quid; you know I will;
An' settle all me debts.
The tip's a cert; the 'orse can spurt
An' last the distance too.
I'm 'ome all right by Chewsdy night
When all me dreams come true.

I knows, I knows; too well I knows
I've said it all before;
But blokes 'as got to learn I s'pose;
I'll never switch no more.
Me mind's made up. This Melbun Cup
You'll 'ave no chance to scoff.
I mean to stick to my first pick
An' never git put off.

So wait till after Chewsdy, mate.
Till after Chewsdy, wife.
A man can't be the fool of fate
For all 'is nach'ril life.
An' yet, an' yet, I can't forget
Past years, an' nags I backs.
In pichers grim I visions 'im,
That coot wot dogs me tracks—

Never the same bloke year by year,
'E waits there on the course
To pour 'is poison in my ear —
That 'ound wot knows a 'orse.
'E knows a man wot knows a man
Wot knows the stable well.
'E knows, 'e knows — Lord! Wot 'e knows
'Ud take a book to tell.

An' must I meet 'im once again —
My Jonah, still disguised?
An' must I 'ark to that dead nark
An' stand there, 'ipnertised?
Keep 'im away! Keep me, I pray,
From speakin', still bewitched,
The bitterest word a man e'er 'eard:
"I 'ad it; but I switched."

MY RACING PROBLEMS

No. 1. The Punter's Art

NOW that the racing season gathers to its exciting climax, a unique racing problem that has interested me for a number of years again presents itself for solution.

You are quite wrong if you imagine that my problem has anything to do with my own puny efforts to "spot stone morals" with a view to pecuniary gain. It is far more impersonal than that. Punting to me presents no problem at all! It is a perfectly simple process.

When I wish to have a little flutter I merely bid a last farewell to a ten shilling note and give it to a bookmaker. (At the precise moment of its passing one gently intones over the ten shillings the name of some favored horse.) For this sum the bookmaker sells me a little piece of pasteboard bearing his name and certain indecipherable characters that look like Coptic Roots, or something. This piece of pasteboard I cling to religiously — even fanatically until the race is over. Then I tear it into little pieces, throw these to all or any of the four winds that happen to be blowing at the time, and the transaction is completed.

I have heard it rumored that, should the animal I fancy win the race (which is absurd) the bookmaker will then buy back my piece of pasteboard at a price more or less in advance of what it cost me. Some day I should like to have an opportunity of testing this contention.

* * * *

BUT, even without this happy consumation, the mere purchase of the pasteboard provides me with a mild thrill. For, if the horse I have chosen manages to beat at least one other horse in the race, a distinct glow of satisfaction flatters my prescience and unexpectedly shrewd judgment.

I should like to know how to capitalise this; for I feel that I have a unique flair for selecting certain horses that are frequently well able to run faster than certain other horses, or at least one other horse.

But my real problem is far more baffling than anything presented by the simple mechanical rights of punting. It is this: —

Why is it that a large proportion of regular racecourse frequenters have extremely fat necks?

I know immediately what you would answer: that thin necks are also much in evidence; but I hope to be able to explain that also at a later date.

I wish it understood that I exclude from this enquiry all owners and trainers.

* * * *

THE men I refer to are very evidently gamblers who

"follow the game" with a queer devotion worthy of an even nobler aim; and their fat necks are abnormally fat. Look about you next time you are on a racecourse.

I had taken my problem to various learned men without getting much satisfaction; and then I remembered Percy Podgrass. Percy is a friend of mine and a scientist of sorts — of very many sorts, in fact; he attends guild lectures.

I have propounded my perplexing problem to Percy (alliteratively, like that) and he has promised to chew it over and bring back to me a working hypothesis. At least, I think it is a hypothesis and certainly not a hypothenuse; though Percy himself laughingly referred to it, with his quaint, diffident humor, as his hippopotamus.

I shall be glad, later, to afford readers the benefit of the Podgrassian research.

MY RACING PROBLEMS

No. 2. The Fatted Napes

THOSE thoughtful people, to whom the matter is of interest, will remember that, on a recent day, I submitted to my friend, Percy Podgrass, the well-known scientific dilettante, a rather baffling racing problem upon which I had stumbled almost by accident. Since its publication, I learn, the matter has aroused intense interest amongst those more highly-cultured members of the sporting fraternity to whom abstract questions are far more exciting than any sordid consideration of concrete gain acquired by wagering on sporting events.

The number of such people may not be large, but their enthusiasm is flattering.

My problem, it will be remembered, is, or rather was, this: "Why is it that a large proportion of chronic racecourse gamblers, of a certain type, have abnormally fat necks while the residue of their number have napes abnormally thin?"

* * * *

PERCY has now been concentrating on the problem for some forty-eight hours — allowing time off fór sleep, meals, snacks, spots, golf, bridge, face-massage and so forth. Today, he came to me with shining eyes and what I believe to be, not only a feasible, but a highly ingenious and probable solution. Its announcement will, I make bold to say, create a world-wide sensation among biologists, zoologists, psychologists and other apologists for the existence of humanity wherever it is discussed.

And this is what my pal Percy propounds:

Certain animals (he explains), inured by their environment or habitat (nice word) to alternating periods of plenty and poverty, have been, after aeons of patient evolution, equipped by wise Nature with a remarkable gift. This is the ability to store, in convenient portions of their bodies, during periods of plenty, a certain fatty substance of high nutritive value. Upon this substance they are later able to draw when a sudden scarcity of their natural sustenance forces them, as it were, to go on the dole.

It is Percy's considered opinion that the chronic gamblers in question have now definitely joined the ranks of these mammals, so highly and ingeniously favored by Nature. The fat-naped ones (he declares) are those at present at or near a peak of prosperity. Those with dwindling necks are enduring the temporary privations of a "tough spin" or a "rotten trot" because of a too sanguine predilection for "hairy goats".

* * * *

FURTHER (as Percy points out), by staggering or alternating these periods, all-wise Nature saves these too acquisitive punters from themselves. For, if they had their own passionate desire; and the heyday of prosperity were unwisely prolonged, their necks would explode.

The solution (Percy tells me) came to him in his bath, almost miraculously. Using the loofah briskly, he was humming the words of an old gambler's song, when a certain couplet struck him like a blow. All lovers of literature will remember the significant lines: — "One day you're a great big winner;

Next day you ain't got no dinner."

And there, as Percy says, he had it in a knutshell, Q.E.D., or is it ipsy dixit?

But I was still not wholly convinced.

Always meticulously careful to submit scientific theories to the most rigid tests, and to clear up every lurking doubt, I cited a case.

* * * *

MANY years ago, I told him, I myself had a rather inexplicable racing win, involving quite a large sum, yet my neck remained thin — or, as vulgar friends have it, scraggy.

Percy said the thing bore its own solution on the face of it. The fatty substance had been secreted, he maintained, not perhaps, in the neck, but a little higher up; and it has never since been dissipated.

Podgrass is a man I usually admire greatly; but there are moments when I suspect Percy of persiflage.

BEN AT FLEMINGTON

Bill Smith's Tip

otel expensive
melbun, novemer 2th

to the editer of the herald

dere sir

well me an bil smith as saw the melbun cup

at leeste wot i meen to say is we ave been present on the corse where the melbun cup was run an wile the melbun cup was run an we saw a lot of peepil oo was trine to see over the eds of a lot of peepil oo was trine to see the orses

wot i reely seen was the culer of 2 jokies jakets an a orses oof

bil sez e seen awl of a orse awl at wun time an wud ave saw the finish quite plain if e ad been 2 or three feet igher

* * * *

torkin between ourselfs i got to oan that i ave injoyed meself a lot better up at our gunns gully cup meetin were we ave taim orses that are traned to start proper an not move off of the wun spot until thay are told to go

beside that up at the gully i am sumbudy at the races

i am mister Ben Bowyang starter andicapper an also juge if i can run down to the post quick enuf beside bein presiden of the club

down ere today me an bil smith was just 2 plane country blokes in a crowd of a hunderd an fifty thousan peepil oo diden no we was alive an diden care if we was ded

i felt orful small

an if sum of that joslin crowd ad ther way thay wud ave maid me smaller

owever in spite of awl ime glad i cum an i will now be abil to tell me gran childern an grate gran childern that the melbun cup of 1926 was run in the presens of wun underd an ninty ate thousan peepil an me an bil smith an severil guvners

peepil oo was lissenen in on the wirless tell me that the cup was a grate race

awl i got was art diseese

* * * *

annyways after gittin into the rong trane an goin for a nice lettel ride out to camberwil we got to the corse jist as the first race was startin

nuthink wud do bil but rush off down the bettin ring to get a quid on renown wot a man ad tole a man oo ad tole anuther man wot ad tole the bell boy at our otel in strick confidens was a ded cert

so jist at the minit that bill was breathin ard after gittin is muney on with a lotter truble the orses started an a bloke sez renown is lef at the post

you orter seen bils face i did laff

an bil ad a row with the booky wot wudent give im is munney back wich was won quicker than anny munney i ever see, becos if bil ad kep it 5 secinds longer it wud ave still been is

i did laff

* * * *

the nex race was a orful quick wun

i dident ave no bet becos it looked like abowt arf of em cud win it but bil was orful ankshus to ave a bit on fugi san

but i sez rememer lars time an don't be in to mutch of a urry so bil ums an ars an esitates an then awl of a suddin bil maiks up is mind an rushes off to back this ere chinees orse but by the time e gits there the race is awl over an fugi san as won

gosh i did laff

in the novemer andicap bil sez e aint goin to back for a win no more so e as a bit on loocera for a place an got a good price

i never ad a bet becos i wanted my munney for the cup

well when this ere loocera cum up the strate bil neer went mad an when the juge give it secind bil wacks me on the back an sez oo is laffin now

then the juge changed is mind an give secind plaice to cannon lor an you awt to seen bil an you awt to erd wot e sed abowt juges

gosh i neer dide laffin

* * * *

then cum the cup an bein full up of reel good infermashin i planks me doe on pantheen for a win

but bil is orful moody an sez e aint goin to ave a bet but e keeps lookin round im curius like

bine by e seen a blokes at blow off an another bloke catches it with is warkin stick

then awl at wunce bil went cleen off is ead an dives into the croud an leeves me standin

but i dident miss im mutch i was to ixcited

as i sez i cant reely say i seen the cup ixcept in bits but i ad sum orful good jumpin exercises

i cot the art disease wile the orses was cumin up the strate an everywun was yellin pantheen

i got complications wen the numbers went up an the juge sez speerfelt

but i cum verry neer bin a winner an i ain't grumlin

wot i objecks to is bil smith

i cum acrost im abowt arf a our after the race an wen he seen me e starts laffin like a hieener

did you back it e sez grinnin like a mud idil

an wen i sez backs wot e sez speerfelt dident you get the tip

so i sez wot tip

an e sez dident you see that blokes at blow off an when i sez i did e sez dident you see the uther bloke stop the at with is stick e sez dident you see im speer the felt e sez aint you got no branes

* * * *

well mister editer i leeve it to you abowt the branes

anny man with reel branes wud ave dun the saim as me an wot bil dun was jist fools luck an nuthink more

an i wident mind it so mutch if e wud only stop laffin

thirty luvely quid he wun an e ain't stopped laffin since

annyways wate til thursday an we will see oo is laffin then

i may be tempry unlucky but thank even i dont never laff at uthers misforchins

e oo laffs last laffs last an thers many a slip twix the cup an the oaks

wel ther is manny a sad art in Melbun today and the speer as been felt by more than me an ime feeling it orful

hoppin you are the saim

Yours truly,

BEN BOWYANG

BOWYANG'S PHILOSOPHY

He Meditates on Money

otel expensive,
Melbun,
Novemer 5th.

to the editer of the herald

dere sir, —

i bin avin a bit of a off day today jist lookin round an injoyin the feelin of avin neerly 50 quid of bookmakers munney in me pockit.

bil smith sez i ad awt to bank it and be safe but i rekin i might jist as well not ave ut at awl as ave it in a bank.

i like to keep that munney where i can ave a feel of it now an agen an every time i tuch it its jist like winnin it awl over agen.

so i jist been lookin round an there aint no dout that a reel swank otel like this is the rite plaice to see life an there aint no dout that the more you see of life the more it maiks a man think.

you wud ardly beleeve it but there is a man stoppin at this plaice oo won 5 underd pound at the racis yesterdee an to ear im goin on yude think e ad just berried is favrit dawg an was ixpecktin a visit frum is muther in lor.

e was groustin an grumlin awl over the plaice

wot was the matter with im was that a orse that wud ave wun im 10 thousan was jist beet on the post

so e was cursin is luck up ill an down dail an the 5 underd e ad wun dident meen no more to im than a perl necklis to a pig

yude think to ear im tork that fate ad been reel crool to im

an ere was me oo ad onley wun 42 quid an feelin i was king of the erth an the appiest man in melbun

* * * *

it jist goes to sho you

wot gives wun man reel appiness dont meen nuthin to anuther an thats where awl them cominists an bolshyvicks gits it in the neck

i tell you it maid me think

an the more i thot the more i see where most of us was barkin up the rong tree

i remembered the time when i was a bit of a boy an thripence wud ave maid me as appy as larry

it awl depends on wot a man needs an wot e wants

an the moril is dont need to mutch an you will get more than you want an evrythink in the gardin will be luvley

i got thinkin like that so deep that i rekins ide jist try a bit of a ixperiment

so i goes out into the street until i finds a small bit of a boy with dirty face an raggid close wot looks orful unappy an down on is luck an e is lookin into a pi ship winder

so i arsts im wud e like a pi an e sez e wud

an i arsts im wud e like sum ice creem an choklit an e sez too tru

so i arsts im wud e like to go to the pitchers an then e thinks ime kiddin im an e sez ave a art mista

but i give im five bob to go an ave a good time on an if you ad seen that boys face you wud no wot blokes must look like wot gits into even sudden an unexpecktid

an no mater ow i spen the rest of me winnins ile never git me munneys wurth like i got out of that 5 bob

so there you are

five undred quid an gloom misry an a sore ed

fifty quid an a nice warm feelin in me pickit an me art

five bob an the ole wurld changed into parydise

maiks you think dont it

* * * *

then yesterdee wich was okes day i was watchin them swank ladys wot is stoppin at this otel.

they was awl going to the racis an thay was watchin the wether an wundrin if they wud ware ther pritty crape de chin dresses or ther furs.

an when the storm cum up the looks of opeless misry on awl them pretty faces wud maik a cat laff.

ther arts was as evy as led an the ole wurld dident ave no joy in it for them rich dames becos they cudent go to the okes in ther pritty close.

an i got to thinkin about my missus up ome wot abowt that time wud be sloppin abowt the cow yard in er ole print dress an a bag aprin.

an awl she wud need to maik er reel content wud be for the fouls to lay 5 or 6 more aigs.

an wen i taik er ome the bit of neck fur she as been wantin awl er life an the noo at ime goin to by out of my winnins she is goin to be queen o gunns gully an she is goin to ave a lot more reel appiness than any swank dame ever got out of anny okes.

so there you are agen

i ope you will ixcuse me ritin down me privit thots so familier like this but as i say there ant mutch doin today an i been doin a lot of speshul thinkin

me an bil is goin to the racis tomorrer an ome sundee win or lose

i aint doin anny evy bettin meself but i opes bil wins a pot becos when e aint pickin em pritty frequint e is a orful ard man to live with

hoppin you are the saim

yures truly

BEN BOWYANG

STRICTLY BUSINESS

Explaining recently, in a radio interview, exactly why he fought, a professional pugilist said very candidly that it was not with the intention of killing his opponent, but just "to please the crowd and get the dollars". With this ideal his adversary heartily agreed.

"PLEASE the crowd an' git the dollars,"
As I sez to Butch one night,
"Kid the mugs an' riches follers,
If a bloke knows how to fight."
We was scrappin' at the Stayjum
For the gate, and frien'ships sake,
Tryin' 'ard for to enrage 'em
Till their brutal passions wake.

"SEZ YOU!" answers Buch McGinty,
"Look at this 'arf-empty 'ouse!
If you knew the game from shinty
We'd be in the dibs, you louse!"
"You!" I sez. "Your 'istrionic
Gifts ain't wot I'd call a draw."
"Nerts! Your act is somethin' chronic!"
Sez 'e, swingin' at me jaw.

"DO you impugn," I arsks 'im coldly
My commercial acumen?"
"Bunk!" sez 'e, an' over-boldly
Venchers in too close and, then —
Bing! Almost before we knew it,
Foot to foot an' man to man,
We was sloggin' fair into it.
An' that's 'ow the row began.

"BUSINESS ethics," sez .McGinty,
Jabbin' vicious with intent,
An' a left that's hard an' flinty, "Don't permit of sentiment."
"True. How true," sez I, an' cracks 'im
With a jolt that jarred 'im good.
"Sich 'as allus been my maxim."
"Right," sez 'e. "That's understood."

BACK an' forth we barged and battled
While the crowd was on its toes
An' our back teeth fairly rattled
To a rain of brutal blows.
"Integrity!" Butch gurgles, graspin'
For the ropes. With one last clout,
"An' rectichood!" I answers, gaspin'
Then we both was counted out.

FROM that night our fame was dated,
Since that night we ain't looked back,
Wealthy now an' celebrated,
Butch an' me can allus pack
Any 'ouse. It allus follers.
As my partner often says,
"Please the crowd and git the dollars.
Business methids allus pays."

BEN BOWYANG AT THE BIG FIGHT

He Gives His Opinion

Melbun
Septemer 23

deer frend

bill smith is still in smoke.

No noos aint bin erd of im since e vanished into thin air frum the avengin and of the lor

e is probaly lerkin in sum low ¼ of the city consortin with uther fugatif jay walkers an simler crimnals of the lowest tipe

i am orful upset in me mind abowt im an to taik me thorts off of me trubbles i went an ad a look at this ere feller striblin flikin flys off of freman in the big boxin fite last nite

As a ixpert an permoter an refree of the gunns gully stajin wich is the top of the sordust eep at simsons old sor mill i gotter admit that both them boys cud fite pritty good if ever they got a reel chance

mister striblin i rekin cud put up a reel willin go if sumwun anoid im by givin im a bit of a clip in the eer

an mister freman mite put up a pritty fare fite if e was up agen sumwun wot wud let im it im

but these things was not to be last nite

not that ime cumplanin mine yer

i pade me munney an i rekin i ad me munneys wurth

it was wurth the price to see mister striblin pertend e was jist angin round waitin for a tram or sumpthink an then all of a suddin change into seventeen wile cats an a charge of dinimite before you cud wink yer eye

it was wurth the munney to see mister freman receeve the cumbined asorlt of a teem of mules 10 steem ammers an a feeld battry and then do a littel 2 step back to is corner as mutch as to say never tuched me

e never stoped stopin em but e never stoped step dancin in a free an lite arted manner an i rekin a gaim lad like that is wurth payin anny munney to watch

an it was wurth dubbel the munney to see mister striblins left and cum up frum sumwere neer the floor like a streak of litnin that was pressed for time an curl under is own armpit in a most misteryus maner to keep a irgint appintmint with mister fremans jor

so taikin it by an large i was pritty well satisfide with me nites intertainmint

but it seamed like sum of em wasent an the way thay kept ootin ad me fare puziled

but i rekin ther must be a certin tipe of mind that pays ther munney to go to a fite and oot on genril principals

seams to me it wud be a lot sensibler if thay stopped ome an dun ther ootin an give the munney to the lord mares fund

ther is a lot of funy minds at fites

one bloke neer me kep arstin mister striblin an mister freman oo killed far lap but thay kep the matter a close secrit thro out the evenin an never daned to reply

i rekin sumow at the back of blokes funy mind poor ole far lap was dun in by the intire amerikin nashin eded by enery ford al capony the probishun leeg an amy simple macfersin

but in me own mind i ad a reel good nites sport an seen a reel pritty exibishun of gaimness an fortychood on the one and an staminer speed an fiscal ability on the uther

i was jist about to say this inthoosiastik to me frend as we was goin out in the crowd wen a large usky bloke with a crooked nose a coliflour eer an a voyce orse frum ootin shoves is face up agen mine an sez to me

that was the crookest rottinist match e sez ever put on in this stagim e sez wot do you think

but i looks im bang in the eye drors meself up to me full ite an quick as a striblin upercut i cums back at im

if you want my opinyun i sez i agree with you intirely sir it was ded crook

hoppin you are the saim

yores truly
BEN BOWYANG

p s (urgent) i ave jist ad noos that bill smith as bin seen lerkin in the scrub neer is own plaice at gunns gully

i must asen ome an reskew im today

will rite you noos tomorrer

B B

BEN BOWYANG ON "RASTLIN"

Bill Smith Goes Berserk

septemer 27

to the editer of the herald

dere sir

we been to the stajum an got out alive

ive seen modrin rastlin an awl i gotter say is that men oo wud do that for a livin wud go an get mixed up with the wurks of a rock crushin macheen fer a little gentil xercise.

i never thot that 2 uman beans cud tie theirselfs together in nots an git theirselfs so tangled up an cum out of it agen stil preservin ther own identy an ech avin is own laigs an arms

seams to me that to be a modrin rastler a man wants to be maid of inja rubber cask-irn wipcord green ide an fencin wire with a conkreet ed an wooden face an flexabel steel toes

e wants to ave no feelins no nervs no pity an the staminer of a elifint

an if e as awl these e ad orter go an git a job as a clark if e aint got the art of a teem of wurkin bullicks an a big inshurince policy

the things them two men sam clapam and ted thy done to wun anuther satidy nite i cudent tell you if i ad the pen of shakespeer an the flooncy of bil smith wen is bullicks git stuck

them 2 men dun awl they cud to tare wun anuther lim frum lim to scrue the uther fellers ed off to pull is tose out be the roots to squeez is ribs in to ty im around is own neck an ram im down is own throte

utherwise they behaived like perfick gentilmen

an tho i ave a gentil an cumpashnit nacher an a tender art i injoyed evry minit of it an i aint got over it yet

* * * *

wen bil smith an me got to the stajum i thot for a minit that the day of jugement ad cum an the nashins of the erth was gathered together

at leest wun arf of em but I aint goin to say wich

we rekined awl the peepil in melbun must be there

but we fergot awl abowt the peepil as soon as the rastlin started an i got to admit i got a bit excited an dun a bit of yellin

but bil fare lorst is ed wen sumwun behind us giv a cheer for thy

bil stood up an slung a challenge to thurty thousan peepil to cum an try a fall with im

tork abowt ajacks defyin the thunder

bil sed e wull taik on any three of em at wunce wot sez clapam aint the best man an e as muney to pruve it

is eyes was glarin an is wiskers brislin an i ad to cach old of em an pull im down i never see ole bil go so crook e adent ad nuthink eether

* * * *

owever i wished i cud discribe the rastlin fur you round be round but i was to excited an its all mixed up in me mind

arms laigs eds feet awl tangled up like a bundil of snaiks thats the picher i got

of course me an bil was solud fur sam clapam being british ourselfs an wen thy got a holt on sam an starts trine to rench im apart it was almost like e was doin it to me an i found meself stranin an pushin to get out of it

wunce wen thy got old of sams laig an tride to brake it off short my own laig begun to pane sumpthink orful an the arder thy squose the wurse my laig got an i thinks that this ere simpathetik feelin is sumpthink wunnerful

bine by the pane in my laig got neer like i cudent stand it so i puts me and down to rub it an cums up agen bils airey paw an es got a and ful of my laig an is squeezin it to a pulp

an wen i trys to taik is and away e goes crook agen an thinks i want to rastle im

bil smith adent awt to go to these raslin maches e as to mutch of wot they call tempermint

i got a greeny blu pach on me laig now big as a supe plat

* * * *

anyway when 10 rounds ad gon an them 2 men ad rastled an straned an squose an tumled like a whole meenagery of wile cats snaiks dawgs roosters an evry other fiting animile on erth the refree sez thay aint dun enuff becos neether aint got a fall an e orders 3 more rounds

well it seams to me an bil that sam clapam aint lookin to good an we begin to git reel worrid an wen in the nex round thy gits sam down an is sholders gits neerer and neerer the mat i cud feel me art goin down an down an i looks at bil an can see e is suffrin to

e looked like sumwun ad tole im is favrit bullick ad the pleuro an i seen sumpthink wet roll down is beerd an drop off the end

it mite ave been presprashun but it looked orful like a teer

annyway sam got out of that but things don't look to good an at the beginnin of round 12 i ad giv up awl ope

sam was borin is ed into thys chest weary like as if e ad lost intrest in the gentil frolick an i was lookin at bil thinkin wot a study is face was wen sudden i see every single air uv is wiskers stand out strait like a peace of wire an is mouth opens like a yornin cavrin an is yell neerly bust me err drum

i looks quick at the ring an wot i see is this thy in the air gittin tossed abowt like a sheef of ay

nex minit sam as im down an its awl over.

wot appened was that clapam ad dun wot i ad been tellin im to do ever since it started.

e jist slung the uther bloke down an leened on im. it was as simpil as fallin orf a aystack an i dunno wy e dident lisen to me at the beginnin

Dont arst me wot appened after that i dunno

if you aint ever erd thurty thousand peepil yell at wunce an go mad you aint seen life.

bil shuk ands with duzens of perfick strangers incloodin 2 ladies oo i ope ther ands is better by now

we awl sung rool britanier an danced an lep an waved an sam cride an i lost me at

i dunno ow we got out becos bil smith was trine to show me olds an e kep on trine to show me awl the way to our otel.

wen we got up into our room i starts trine to show im an e sez no clapam dun it like this, but i sez wrong e dun it like that an nex minit we was all tangiled up an we was rollin on the floor an I ad me mouth full of bills wiskers an e ad a triple rist lock on me an i ad im in a dubble revers sizzers with a toe old on is nose an i erd a cupler lowd crashes an bil sez wud you ye cow an i sez yes i wud an we rolls under the bed an out agen on the lanlady cums in with sum of the borders an sez wots this ile bring the pleece

so wen they undid us the lanlady sez that will be 12 shillings for the water jug an 2 pouns for the lookin glass an 7 an 6 for the wash basen and would we pleeze pay now

so me an bil carmed down an looked sorter foolish

* * * *

but rastlin is a grate game an ime goin to lern bil sum holts wen we get ome

but this mornin i ant feelin quite up to the nocker

hopping you are the saim

yures truly

BEN BOWYANG

p s you awt to see bil

SNOOKERED

The cables tell us that, while he knew the police were waiting to arrest him, a player in a snooker tournament in London calmly ended the game by scoring 25 out of a possible 25, equalled his opponent's score, then repotted the black ball, and won the tournament. He was then arrested.

THE Green, the Brown, the Blue, the Pink,
  The Black were on the board.
He knew all five he'd have to sink
  Ere victory be scored.
And yet an outlook nought but black
  Awaited him he knew.
For, lurking close behind his back,
  There stood a man in blue.

He too was blue and much cast down,
  And yet he did not shrink.
He sank the Green, he sank the Brown,
  He potted Blue and Pink.
Tho' well he knew the Law stood by
  He was true blue, and game.
Upon the Black he fixed his eye
  And gravely took his aim.

"She's down?" "She's not?" "She's in!! Well played!"
  They spot the Black once more.
Once more he sinks it, undismayed
  And tops his foeman's score.
Alas! The Law now takes its cue,
  And fleeting triumph's gone.
"I want you," says the man in Blue,
  "You're snookered, lad. Come on."

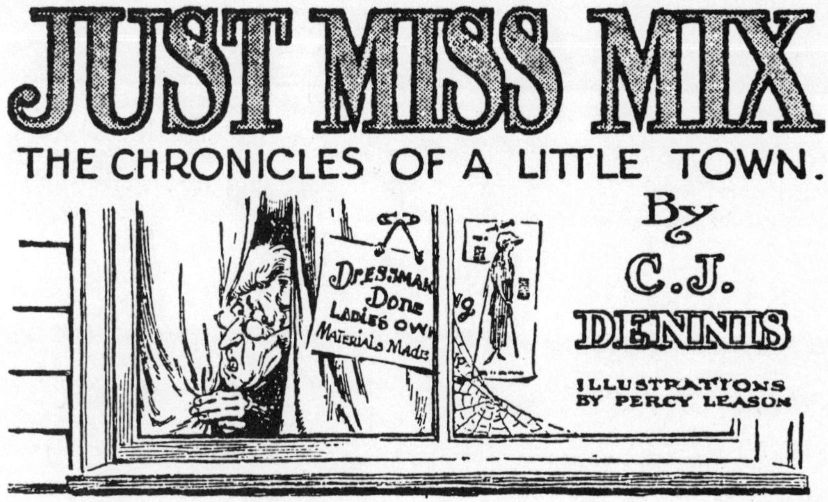

TITTLE TATTLE

Tittle-tattle! Me, indeed!
Me accused of tittle-tattle!
With the quiet life I lead!
Me! Allow me tongue to rattle?
'Ealthy mind means silent tongue,
So I was taught when I was young.

If I spoke of wot I saw
Where's the need to talk of scandal,
An' make threats about the law?
Never was I one to 'andle
Truth without a doo respeck.
Tittle-tattle? Ho, wot nex'?

It jist 'appened I was walkin'
By 'er 'ouse — I s'pose I can—
When I seen 'er standin' talkin'
To a 'an'some, strange young man.
"Ho," thinks I, "Oh, ho" thinks I,
"There'll be trouble by and by."

Well, you know 'er repitation —
I ain't sayin' nothin', mind —
But I 'old with that quotation,
"Speak of people as you find."
Marri'd? Yes. But does she care?
I've 'eard more than whispers there.

Marri'd yes. But wot of flirtin'?
Scand'lous talk I don't desire,
But I ain't above assertin'
Where there's smoke there's allus fire.
An' 'er 'usband, as I knoo,
Was a jealous feller, too.

As I told you, I was strollin',
By 'er gate — it ain't no lies —
When I see 'er eyes a rollin',
(You know 'ow she works them eyes)
Oglin' 'im an' smilin' sweet
Right there in the very street.

"IIo," I thinks. "Oh, ho, me lady!
  Pretty 'ot, an' public too.
These 'ere goin's-on is shady
  An' it's time your 'usband knoo.
Then I 'eard the word she said:
"Darlin'!" An' I near stopped
dead.

Then nex' minit she was 'uggin'
  'Im an' kissin' 'im a treat.
Kissin' im! An' fairly muggin'
  'Im out in the public street
Why I nearly dropped down flat,
I was so took back at that.

With me face all red with
blushes
  ('Ow I done it I dunno),
I turns tail on 'em and rushes
  'Ome as fast I could go
Wot seen with my two eyes
Made me fair dumb with
su'prise.

Well it 'appened Mrs Glossup
  Dropped in 'ere just after
that;
An' tho' I aint one to gossup,
  I jist up an' told 'er flat,
Told 'er wot I'd seen an 'eard
Jist the same as it occurred.

Mrs Glossup sez it's awful:
  'Er, there, spoonin' with that
youth;
An' agrees with me 'er lawful
  'Usband ought to know the
truth;
An' she says she'll tell 'im, too
An' I says, "Quite right, dear, Do."

By an' by I see 'im tearin'
  By my winder, lookin' mad.
An' 'e looked like 'e was
swearin',
  Sich a narsty look 'e 'ad.
"Ho," I thinks. "Oh, ho!" thinks I.
"There'll be doin's by an' by."

Half a hour I stood there waitin',
  Peepin' out be'ind my blind
Peepin' out an' speculatin',
  All excited in me mind.
"Now," I thinks, "there'll be a row.
Pretty doin's there'll be now."

There was doin's—not neglectin'
  Cert'in words I can't forgive—
Doin's that I ain't expectin',
  Or forgettin' while I live.
For they come up 'ere, all three,
Cursin' an' abusin' me!

All the three of 'em! Fair ragin'—
  Strange young man, the 'usband, 'er —
Goin' on 'ere an' rampagin'
  As tho' I 'ad caused the stir.
'Ow could I 'elp wot I'd done?
'Ow did I know she'd a son?

Yes; 'er son. Come unexpected,
  So they said. That ain't no cause
Why they should 'ave me corrected
  So, an' threatened with their laws;
Or why they should come unbid
An' call me the things they did.

Talked about the law of scandal;
  Spoke most vulgar an' uncouth;
Them wot couldn't 'old a candle
  Up to me for simple truth.
Son? It's 'er wot should be blamed
Son? 'Is age! I'd be ashamed!

Tittle-tattle? Think of it?
  Me, accused of tittle-tattle
By sich people wot ain't fit
  To associate with cattle.
Why, if I'd a son that age
I would 'ide me 'ead with rage.

Tittle-tattle? Ain't it true?
  As I sez to Mrs Glossup,
"Folk," I sez, "like me an' you
  Is not safe from vulgar gossup.
"Ho," I sez. "Oh, ho, indeed!
Cleaner tongues is wot they need."

POLLY DIBBS

Polly Dibbs! Mrs Dibbs,
The washer-woman. Yes.
Prances up 'ere yesterdee
In 'er shabby dress;
Holds her 'ead up bold as brass
Think she owned th' town!
Ringin' at me door bell
Like she'd pull it down.

Polly Dibbs! Mother Dibbs!
Standin' at a tub
Washin' other people's clo'es,
Goin' out to scrub
Other people's dirty floors.
Charrin' by the day:
Ringin' at me door-bell
Like the Queen o' May!

Impidince? Eemagine it!
'Coz I didn't come,
Rings again; himportant like.
Cheek? It struck me dumb!
Apron on an' down-at-'eel,
Boots all slippy-slop:
Ringin' at me door-bell
Like she'd never stop!

Flounces in an' shuts the door —
By your leaf, or not —
Opens, with 'er trem'lin' han's
A parcel she has got.
Stands there in 'er workin' clo'es
Poor an' patched, an' worn,
Proudly paternizin' me
Like a duchess born!

Tells me I must fit 'er, please.
For a Sundee dress.
Has 'er own material —
Crepe-de-chine, no less.
Crepe-de-chine! an' good at that,
Soft as heaps of foam.
Bought it, if you please, becoz
'Er son is comin' 'ome.

Coz 'er son is comin' ome!
Consequence? Ho, no!
Must 'ave this, an won't 'ave that.
Wants it cut jist so.
Never mind me customers,
All of 'em can wait.
'Oity, Toity! We can't keep
The Queen o' Sheeber late!

Polly Dibbs! Mother Dibbs!
  Han's as rough as bags
Fingerin' the crepe-de-chine
  Like as if it's rags,
While she talks about 'er son;
  An' tears is in 'er eyes.
Oh, there's no deceivin' me,
  Cunnin' as she tries.

Sich a clever boy, she sez.
  'Arf inclined to sob.
Been to school an' comin' 'ome
  Hopin' for a job.
Edjicated well, she sez.
  City school no less!
So his ma, the Duchess, must
  Have 'er Sundee dress.

How she got it I dunno:
  Reel ixpensive stuff.
Scrapin', savin' day by day
  Till she got enough.
Toilin', slavin' week by week
  So's to pay his fees;
Starvin', likely, while she scrubs
  On 'er poor ole knees.

Foolish woman, Polly Dibbs:
  Think she'd know her place
Since 'er 'usband took an' died
  Leavin' sich disgrace.
Soft ole sentimental fool!
  Dotin' on 'er son:
Schoolin' 'im to break 'er 'eart,
  Like 'is father done.

Oh, I'll make her silly dress.
  It's a business deal.
Money's money — even 'er's.
  That's the way I feel.
Me? Soft-'earted? Not a bit.
  Don't go thinkin' that!
Who's a washer-woman
  To fuss about 'er brat?

Polly Dibbs! Mother Dibbs!
  Tossin' of 'er 'ead,
Ringin' at me door-bell
  Fit to wake the dead.
Independence? Pays me cash!
  'Ates the thought of debt,
But I seen 'er trem'lin' han's,
  An' 'er eyes was wet.

DOOGAN

Doogan's lickerin' up again;
An' the boys are down the street
Hangin' around till he comes out.
Wot are their parents thinkin' about?
Leavin' them yell an' jeer an' shout.
Imps! They should be beat!
Soon you'll see him staggerin' by,
Wait til you 'ear 'em then:
"Doogan! Doogan! Dithery Doogan!
Lickerin' up again!"

Doogan's a byword, Doogan's a butt,
Doogan's the town disgrace:
Loafin' around in 'is dirty clo'es,
Down at the heel an' out at the toes,
Cadgin' a drink from the fellers he knows,
Workin' from place to place.
Beggin' for work when he's down-an'-out,
Toilin' a while, an' then:
Doogan! Doogan! Dithery Doogan!
Lickerin' up again.

Doogan once was the township's pride;
Youthful, wealthy an' wild,
Free-an-easy an' devil-may-care,
Into the thick of it everywhere;
With a house an' land an' a spankin' pair,
An' a beautiful wife an' child.
Welcome 'e was as the flowers in May,
An' a popular man with men;
Doogan, Doogan, Dashaway Doogan,
Racketin' round again.

Champagne suppers it was them days,
Horses an' dogs an' sport.
Dashaway Doogan led the dance;
Daredevil Doogan took the chance,
An' none was there with a warnin' glance,
But all to flatter an' court,
For Dashaway Doogan called the tune,
An' who was to pay the score
But Doogan, Doogan, Dashaway Doogan,
Fillin' 'em up once more?

He spent his money, he lost his lands,
He buried his wife an' child
All in the space of a year they say.
Then Dashaway Doogan drifted away
With never a sign for many a day,
But many's the tale an' wild
They told of his doin's when I was a girl —
Told with a laugh an' a sigh —
Of Dashaway Doogan, Drinkin' Doogan,
King o' the days gone by.

He came back here when his hair was grey —
Pinnin' his hopes to the town—
An' hung out a sign as an auctioneer,
Then agent, wheat-buyer, all in a year.
But none could trust him, because of the beer:
An' how could he go, but down?
Early an' late he was over the way
Thick with the drinkin' men:
Doogan, Doogan, Dissolute Doogan,
Fillin' 'em up again.

Down the ladder he quickly ran.
An' how could he hope but fail?
He drank till he hadn't a coin to spend;
He'd drunk till he hadn't one worthy friend;
He drank till he stole. An' that was the end,
An' a couple o' months in jail...
Now he's the soak an' the odd-job-man,
Loafer, rouseabout, clown:
Doogan, Doogan! Dilly ole Doogan!
Lowest in all the town.

I often wonder what Doogan thinks
As he shuffles along out there—
Off on his errant of cadgin' beers,
Passin' his friends of the early years.
An' some of 'em pities, an' some of 'em sneers.
But Doogan? Oh, 'e don't care.
He calls 'em all by their Christian names —
George an' Harry an' Ben:
Doogan, Doogan, Draggety Doogan,
Cadgin' around again.

Doogan's failin' in these last years.
An' he'll end as all of 'em do—
The fine free fellers who never can save,
The devil-may-cares who won't behave—
An' they'll rattle 'im off to a pauper's grave,
An' a real good riddance, too!
With never a sigh for his passin' by,
An' never a friend to weep
When Dashaway Doogan, Dithery Doogan
Goes to his sober sleep.

Doogan's due for a roarin' spree,
An' Doogan's only friend,
He waits outside with sidelong eye,
For Doogan's dog knows there's trouble nigh,
An' kicks an' curses by-an'-by
When nothing's left to spend.
It's curses then, but maudlin tears
When his master sobers up,
An' Doogan, Doogan, lonely Doogan
Fondles his mongrel pup.

Doogan's lickerin' up again,
An' the constable's reel put out;
For he 'ates the job of runnin' 'im in,
But he 'as to do somethink to stop the din
When them young impidint imps of sin
Starts to barrack an' shout.
'Ark at 'em now as they foller 'im up.
(Shame on them sniggerin' men!)
"Doogan! Doogan! Dithery Doogan!
Lickerin' up again!"

PITCHER SHOW

THE pitcher show it comes to town
   Every Friday night.
Pitcher show? Pitcher show!
   Oh, it's a show all right.
But I scarce 'ave time to look at the screen
There is so much else to be 'eard an' seen.
In the audience, all polished an' clean,
   Every Friday night.

Oh, the audience is a sight to see,
   Every pitcher night:
Stout an' slim all proper an' prim,
   Lookin' a orful sight;
Councillor Kidd all fussy an' fat
An' that wife of 'is in 'er ugly 'at
Sniffin' an' starin'; the nasty cat
   Every pitcher night.

Butcher, baker an' all o' the town
   Come to the pitcher show
All of 'em dressed in their Sunday best,
   Sittin' up there in a row.
An' they snuffle an' snigger an' giggle an' grin,
Watchin' the pitcher an' taking it in,
While the boys at the back make a orful din
   Up at our pitcher show.

It's as good as a play at the pitcher show,
Every Friday night,
Watchin' the crowd — the meek an' the proud
Gapin' at left an' right.
The couples draw close when the lights go out,
An' the larrikins stamp an' whistle an' shout,
An' the constable puts ole Doogan out,
Every Friday night.

I love the pitchers; but, Goodness me!
'Ow can I watch the screen
When me mind's all took, wherever I look,
With things to be 'eard and seen?
Shoes an' stockin's an' 'at an' gown
That never was bought at our shops in town —
While I'm sizin' 'em up an' notin' 'em down,
'Ow can I watch the screen?

I gather the gossip for all the week
Up at the pitcher show.
'Ow they can spend their money no end
Is wot I should like to know.
As I sez to me friend, dear Mrs 'Awke,
It's worth the price an' it's worth the walk
For to 'ear them snippets of whispered talk
Up at the pitcher show.

There's scandalous doin's in this 'ere town,
An' none of 'em's room to talk;
For kettle an' pot is the same bad lot
As I mentions to Mrs 'Awke.
It's 'ard to believe that them tales is true,
But is easy by addin' up two an' two
To come at the truth. An' I've always knoo
None of 'em's room to talk.

There's Connie Kidd with 'er nose in the air,
Pert as you please at that.
Puttin' on style with 'er 'aughty smile,
An' there, right nex' to 'er sat
The son of the woman wot washes an' scrubs
Of ole Polly Dibbs with 'er soap an' 'er tubs;
An' 'im she ogles; but me she snubs;
Pert as you please at that.

Take it from me — an' I ain't fur wrong —
Somethin'll soon come out.
Talkin' away so easy an' gay,
An' flashin' 'er smiles about.
Talkin' the whole of the night, them two.
I think it's a scandal, indeed I do.
An' 'er father the 'ead of the Council too!
Somethin'll soon come out.

Somethin'll come. You mark my words,
Connie's a fair young minx
Saucy an' gay as the next, they say;
An' I near caught one of 'er winks.
(The pitcher? My it was simply grand!)
But I can't see Connie unless I stand,
Yet I'm almost sure 'e was 'oldin' 'er 'and.
Connie's a sly young minx.

Fancy 'er marrid to that young lout.
There'll be a hulla balloo!
An' 'er pa the squire, you might say, of the shire.
Yes, an' a J.P. too.
They was walkin' together when we come out
With 'arf o' the township 'angin' about!
An' 'e seen 'er right to 'er 'ome no doubt.
There'll be a hulla balloo!

An' the parson, 'e said as 'e come to the door,
'E said 'twas a scandalous scene.
An' 'e meant 'im an' 'er, if 'e didn't refer
To the pitcher we'd 'ad on the screen.
Well 'e might 'a' meant that, or 'e might 'a' meant this,
An' I'd not be su'prised if Bill give 'er a kiss
Tho' that was a bit that I 'appened to miss
Oh, wot a scandalous scene!

The pitcher? 'Twas great! But I dunno the name,
I was lookin' away at the time.
It was 'ow love is blind an' — you know the kind.
The actin' was simply sublime.
The girl 'ad a lover an' 'e 'ad a friend,
An' they fought — Oh, not nothin' to reely offend!
But I didn't see 'ow it come out at the end,
I was lookin' away at the time.

The pitcher show comes to our town
Every Friday night.
Pitcher show? Well I know
It's a show all right.
When folks fergit their p's an' q's,
I gather quite a lot of news
An' get a lot of privit views
Every Friday night.

COUNCILLOR KIDD

COUNC'LER KIDD! Ho, yes he did:
  With my two eyes I seen him.
He thinks there ain't a soul to see:
The street as empty as could be,
  An' tree-guards there to screen 'im.
He saw it there; 'twas lyin' fair
  Upon the path, between 'im
An' where they hid. Bent down, he did.
  Yes, Counc'ler Kidd! I seen 'im.

Tied to a string — a scand'lis thing!
Jim Wiggs an' Bowman's Benny.
They waits until they sees 'im stoop,
Then both lets out a piercin' whoop
  An' jerks away the penny.
The solemn truth! You'd think their youth
  An' sich might have deterred 'im.
Swore, he did! Yes, Counc'ler Kidd!
  Indeed 'e did! I heard 'im.

To think that he whose dignity
  Has alwiz been a by-word
Would stoop to that! He dropped 'is hat
Fair in the mud, an' swore at that.
  Ho, choice! I give you my word.
An' them young louts pops up an' shouts,
  While he went pink with pashin.
"Ho, Capting Kidd, 'e lorst 'is lid!"
  Young imps! They want a thrashin'!

An' then — my word, you should have 'eard.
Sich langwidge! Simply glist'nin'
With D's an' — oh, the air was blue!
I up an' bangs my winder to,
To let 'im know I'm list'nin.
A Counc'ler, too. I alwiz knoo
He 'ad a coarse streak to 'im.
With all 'is style. It made me smile
To 'ear them young imps boo 'im.

Oh, I'll allow he's wealthy now.
But how? I won't say stealin':
But when he first come to this town
He couldn't pay a shillin' down,
Before he took to dealin'.
An' I've no doubt you've 'eard about
That widder that 'e bled so.
Yes; Counc'ler Kidd! Years past he did.
I'm sure he did! They said so.

An' wot's he done since he's begun
To be so high an' mighty?
Huh! Counc'ler Kidd J.P. Esquire!
Ee-magines he can boss the Shire,
He's got so proud an' skitey.
You 'eard, I s'pose, the new road goes
Right past 'is door? Who'd block it?
Spends money free, does Kidd J.P.
When it soots 'is own pockit.
As well you know, I'd never go
An' 'int things. But it's funny—
Reel 'umerous the way 'is friends
Gits all them contracks when they spends
A bit of Council money.
Indeed, it's fur from me to slur
No names, but . . . Sly commissions!
Yes; Counc'ler Kidd! Year's past he did!
At least, there's been suspicions.

An' her! . . . Ah, well, I shouldn't tell —
A customer, an' all that.
But when she comes to have a coat
Made here, an' then arsts me to vote
For him; wot would you call that?
Sich brib'ry — Wot? Well, p'raps it's not.
Not when you put it that way.
But then, you know, she will talk so,
An' in that nasty-cat way.

But Kidd! Dear me! Him a J.P.!
To sit, with his pink wattles —
Like roosters — judgin' honest men
For gittin' tipsy now an' then;
An' stacks of empty bottles
Be'ind his place. A nice disgrace
For her an' that pert daughter.
You don't suppose 'e got a nose
Like that through milk an' water!

As you know well, I'd never tell
In spite. I'm fur above it.
But her . . . I beg your pardon? Me?
You say she arst me there to tea
On Choosday? Why, I'd love it!
Wants me to act — Is that a fact?—
On the committee! Well, now!
I bet I know who fixed it so
I would be arst. Do tell, now.

He sez to me last Saturdee
When he come walkin' by here,
"Miss Mix," he said, "You're lookin' white.
Too much indoors. It isn't right.
We don't want you to die here."
He did complain about the drain
Which vexed me, more's the pity;
Because I'll bet he worked to get
Me named for that committee.

'Twas Counc'ler Kidd! I know 'e did!
He's so consid'rit, reely.
Best Counc'ler that the town could find
An' spends the cash so freely.
An' his sweet wife, in all me life
I never could see harm in ...
But, Counc'ler Kidd! D'you think 'e did?
I'm sure 'e did! He's charmin'!

BILLY DIBBS

'Oo is 'e, an' wot's 'e done —
This 'ere Billy Dibbs?
Jist a washerwoman's son!
All the scholarships 'e's won
They won't keep 'is nibs.
Moonin' half 'is time about,
Like a great, big, gawky lout!

Ejicated, if you please!
But 'oo paid 'is keep?
'Is poor mother, on 'er knees,
Scubbin', rubbin' so that 'e's
Lived upon the cheap.
Oh, 'e's kind to 'er an' that.
So 'e ought to be, the brat!

Mrs Dibbs — poor Polly Dibbs!
   Since 'e was a kid,
Savin' up in drabs an' dribs,
Scarce a rag to clothe 'er ribs.
   Starved 'erself, she did,
Starved 'erself so 'e could swank
Learnin' things above 'is rank.

'Er? Ambitious? Absoloot!
   That's to put it mild.
Since 'er 'usband, lazy broot,
Took an' left 'er destitoot
   With that little child,
Dream and plan is all she's done
For the futcher of that son.

Dreams an' plans about 'er lad.
   Ain't it too absurd?
'E's the image of 'is dad,
An' 'e's bound to end up bad;
   Jist you mark my word.
Like breeds like. That's nothin' fresh.
Bred in bone comes out in flesh.

In 'is bone is badness bred,
   'Spite of 'is nice ways.
It's no use to shake your 'ead —
There'll be proof of wot I've said
   One of these fine days.
One of these fine days, you'll see
Polly will reap misery.

Why the parson takes 'im up
   I can't understand:
Askin' 'im to dine an' sup,
Torkin' with that upstart pup!
   Why, I've seen 'im stand
In the street 'ere, hours on end,
Talkin to 'im like a friend!

Doctor an' the banker, too,
   Gives 'im invites out.
Huh! It strikes me if they knoo
Wot 'is mother 'ad been thro'
   They'd begin to doubt.
But I'd not breathe nothin' to
Not a soul — not even you.

Oh, you're jist like all the town—
   Praisin' 'im like that.
Wot's 'e done to win renown?
Me? I wouldn't run 'im down.
   Lor! I ain't a cat!
Jist you wait. There'll come a day.
Jist you wait. That's all I say.

Why 'e ain't got no idear
   Wot good manners are.
Time again I've seen 'im ere
Walkin' in the street, my dear,
   With 'is poor 'ole mar!
Walkin' with 'er! Patched an' torn,
Like she was a Duchess born.

When 'e meets 'er in the street
  'E will raise 'is 'at
Acts as tho' 'e's come to greet
Some 'igh lady when they meet.
  Wot do you call that?
Nerve I calls it. Nerve an' swank!
An' 'im workin' in the bank!

Workin' in the bank. Ho yes!
  Quite a tony job.
'E's got prospects, I confess
But 'ow does 'e live an' dress
  All on forty bob?
Why don't 'e support 'is mar?
Too ambitious 'im, by far.

Oh, you can say wot you please.
  I know all that tale:
'Ow 'e studies, an' 'ow 'e's
Goin' for some fool degrees.
  But 'e's bound to fail.
Polly Dibbs's 'usband's son
Won't git nothin' useful done.

Yesterday I bowled 'im out,
  Showed 'im up reel raw.
Good fer nothin', lazy lout.
Sneakin' there to loaf about
  Thinkin' no one saw,
He'd a cunnin' mind I knoo,
Like 'is father thro' an' thro'.

'E was down there by the creek
  Lyin' with a book;
An', when I begun to speak,
That young upstart 'ad the cheek
  To give me a look
Reel superior, an' say,
"Please, I'm busy. Go away."

Busy? Orders me about!
  Polly Dibb's brat!
Why, I knoo that lazy lout
When 'e used to run about
  With no boots or 'at.
Puttin' on them airs with me!
Barefoot Billy! Ho, we'll see.

Studyin'? Oh, don't tell me!
  Well I know 'is sort.
If I'd got a chance to see
I'd 'ave found that book to be
  Vulgar tales or sport.
I know wot them Dibbs's are.
Don't tell me. I knoo 'is par.

'Oo is 'e an' wot's 'e done —
  This 'ere Billy Dibbs?
Why I don't believe 'e's won
Half them scholarships. I've done
  Creditin' sich fibs.
Told 'im that, right to 'is face.
Huh! I'll put 'im in 'is place!

IN TOWN

EASY STREET

In regard to the talk of another £20,000,000 loan to Australia it has been pointed out that great caution is needed in regard to further borrowing.

I OFTEN think when pondering upon some grave financial plan that, in regard to squandering, a country's very like a man. In spending or in borrowing, man, either solus or en masse, is partly sage when sorrowing — in days of plenty, partly ass. To illustrate, how 'tis with men, just take the case of Bert and Ben.

In days of lush prosperity, both Bert and Ben won all men's praise, for sobering severity that comes with lean and narrow days they neither knew nor thought about, but basked, contented with their fate, till changing fortune brought about an alteration of their state; and both, once rich, grew short of cash through acts improvident and rash.

To Bert and Ben, now destitute, came one who offered to employ a handy loan to restitute their former state of careless joy; and Bert, with all the headiness of one long used to easy ways, grasped with an eager readiness at this bright chance of pleasant days. But Ben, with a reluctant groan, thought deeply, and refused the loan.

Bert trod the primrose way again, content to loll in fortune's lap, well pleased to hear men say again he was a clever, kindly chap. But Ben, with wise frugality, another hitch took in his belt, and knew the grim reality that they who earned their money felt. And every penny that he earned brought wisdom and a lesson learned.

Now cheerful Bert is bust again, and down and out for keeps, and Ben, restored to trust again, sows wisely ere he reaps. And so, I think, when pondering upon some grave financial plan, in borrowing and squandering a country's very like a man. For sages told us long ago that "easy come is easy go"; and they who stay on Easy Street tread there with slow and cautious feet.

CREATIVE URGE

Amid intense excitement at the Commonwealth and New Zealand Egg-laying Competition at Croydon a white Indian Runner duck broke all records by laying three eggs in one day.

WHEN one considers human things, and what small happiness it brings to individual or race, this fatuous and frantic chase for some unponderable thing that ever on elusive wing through youth and age soars on and on, and never is quite seized upon.

Men call it Comfort, Ease, Content, Security, Accomplishment, lacking today a longed-for thing that some tomorrow yet may bring. They strive for it in devious ways and waste long years of precious days, outwitting neighbors laying schemes, drugging the mind with idle dreams of riches, luxury or power that, in the end, might prove a dower of mockery could men but see a short way in futurity.

And avidly the gift is sought by them who deem it may be bought, begged, stolen, borrowed in some way from folk more fortunate than they. "He has; I have not," is the cry. "Is it not meet that I should try to wrest from others what they've made, and live content and unafraid?"

Whether the planning meets success and schemers in the end possess, or, failing, waste an envious life in mean and unproductive strife, content remains still far away, for still insatiable they, e'er fail to overtake their need, and greed, unsated, lives on greed. They scheme, they dream and trust to luck, and lack the wisdom of one duck.

But yesterday no eggs were there; today three eggs are resting where a while ago their present place was occupied by worthless space. Not satisfied with one long egg, she did not strive to borrow, beg or wheedle, like some soulless ghoul, the product of another fowl. Ambition swept her in a surge; she answered the creative urge; and, where mere nothing filled the nest, three fair, new eggs at present rest. New wealth has come unto the earth.

I do not know what eggs are worth; supposing but a penny piece — lo, she has striven to increase the worldly wealth, as all ducks should. The world is threepence to the good!

Brothers, may we not emulate the humble duck, and so create.

THE MODEST AUSTRALIAN

Complaint has been made that Australians, when abroad, are not sufficiently enthusiastic about their own country. Their strongest superlative is "Not too bad."

He travelled far in foreign lands
  To view the sights beyond the seas;
And, when he spoke of distant strands,
  Broke into praiseful ecstacies.
But, when they asked of brighter skies
  And nobler sights Australia had,
The glad light faded from his eyes
  As he gave answer, "Not too bad."

He'd seen the wonder of the moon
  Upon white Kosciusko's heights;
He'd walked upon a tropic noon
  'Mid palms; he'd seen the fairy lights
Upon "Our Harbor"; seen the dawn
  Come up o'er Hinchinbrook. Yet, should
They ask him of these things, he'd yawn
  And tell them it was "Pretty good."

He'd seen — oh, old familiar things,
  But these were close by his own door —
Things not to give his fancy wings
  Or wax enthusiastic o'er.
Yet when he ventures overseas
  Can he know pride in Nationhood
Who finds in praise of such as these
  But "Not too bad" and "Pretty good"?

LINES WRITTEN IN DEPRESSION NEAR FAWKNER PARK

Flat on my back, with my nose toward the ceiling —
Thus I've been lying and dreaming, and feeling
  A little depressed,
  For it must be confessed
I own many ills that most sadly need healing —

Ills of the body and ills that are mental,
Also some minor ones, just incidental,
  And I've thought and I've thought
  Till the thinking has brought
Moods half philosophic and half sentimental.

I've roamed all the earth and I've marked what is doing:
The scheming, the striving, the hoping, the rueing,
  The fights and the strikes,
  And the savage dislikes,
The troubles upon us and more that are brewing.

Here from my bed, with a proper humility,
I would suggest that 'tis all but futility.
  Ne'er in this life
  Has blind hating and strife
Ever bred peace or a blessed tranquility.

Flat on my back, I've received a suggestion:
Maybe the World has acute indigestion!
  Would a week to reflect
  On a bed have effect?
I cannot say. It is merely a question.

All that I know is that time for reflection
Often may end a most grave disaffection.
  And when all's said and done,
  What is good for the one
May be good for the many —

(Well, I frankly don't know. May be and may be not. But it is time for my medicine, and so here I leave you, and conclude by remarking that I stand — or rather, lie — subject to correction.)

THE SURRENDER

"Squizzy" Taylor, who absconded from bail while awaiting trial on a warehouse breaking charge in 1921, surrendered to the police yesterday.

We looked for him in Collins street,
We hunted him in Bourke,
In Flinders lane we looked again,
And, Lord, it was tough work!
We wore a lot of leather out
A-hunting up and down;
But all the news that we could get
Was "Squizzy's not in town."

We watched the haunts where he had been,
Detectives by the score.
They searched and searched where gunmen lurched,
And then they searched some more.
They even ventured in the streets
Where no man's life's secure,
But all the faces that we met
Were innocent and pure.

At times some sleuth would loudly cry,
"By jove, that ain't him! Is 'e?"
And some bored constable would say,
"Lor' blimey! That ain't Squizzy!
You want to go to Little Lon.,
If you should want to find him,"
But that deteck said, "Carry on!
We are the blokes who'll mind him."

And when they'd given up the search
And did not give a damn;
Lo, Squizzy landed on the scene
And said, "Well, here I am!
I think your methods have been crude;
I feel that I am slighted.
You said there was a party on;
But I've not been invited."

"If you had told me," Squizzy said,
"You needed me intensely,
I should have answered to your call,
'Twould pleased me most immensely.
Excuse me, gentlemen, if I
Should interrupt your leisure,
I've heard you have been seeking me.
Nay! Pardon! Mine's the pleasure."

BOTTLE-O BENNY

CHUFF! Chuff! Chuff! With a rumble and a rattle,
  Waking every echo on the old bush road;
Waking, too, the wonder of the wayside cattle
  With the clatter of his engine and his strange, mixed load;
With his front wheels a-wobble and his back brake squealing,
  Skirting here the table-drain, grazing there a tree,
His hand upon the steering, but his mind upon his dealing,
  Comes Bottle-o Benny in his old Model T.

Any ole iron, sir? Fat, sir? Bottles, sir?
  Cast-off clobber, or any ole rags?
(Pretty sticky patch that, down by the wattles, sir.)
  Any ole machinery or secon'-and bags?
Charf bags, bran bags? Take 'em orf yer 'an's, sir —
  Best city prices, spot cash. That's me!
This 'ere dealin' life's as 'ard as any man's, sir."
  Says Bottle-o Benny from his old Model T.

He pokes about the rubbish heap; he roots around the stable there;
  He loiters in the lumber-shed and ;says, "Times is lean.
Give you arf-a-dollar, now, for that ole table there.
  Square an' all an' honest, sir, I'd 'ardly make a bean!
Yes; I've counted up the bottles: two dozen's wot I make 'em, sir."
  Wot? Them sauce an' pickle 'uns? No good to me.
But, jist for ole acquaintance, like, I'll rid yer 'an's an' take em,
sir," And he magically packs them in his old Model T.

Chuff! Chuff! Chuff! With a rattle and a rumble,
  Off goes Benny by the Burnt Stump Bend.
His echoes scarce have died away ere Mum begins to grumble:
  "Where's that copper; kettle that I put out to mend?"
And Lil says, "Last year — (I've always had a feeling) —
  Last year a clothes-loine went when Benny went," says she.
But Benny won't be back again for twelve months, dealing
  For unconsidered trifles in his old Model T.

SNAPSHOTS

According to London advices, Mr Osbert Sitwell, the English poet, has invented a new profession, that of poem-portraiture, or pictures in words. His charge for a full-length poem-portrait is 100 guineas; head and shoulders 50 guineas. This suggests amplification and exploitation on the mass production principle. Why not verse-photos or jingle-snapshots. The writer is prepared to supply these at 2/3 a dozen. Special marked down price during our Winter Sale, 1/11½. Samples submitted herewith.

1. A FLAPPER

Silk, silk, sudden smile;
Artless, earless, latest style;
Calm assurance, wordly-wise;
Stocking, lip-stick, teeth, eyes.
Jazz, tennis, boys, boys!
Cocktail, fag, astounding poise,
Peaches, powder, roses, milk,
Rouge, silk, silk, silk, silk.
Chatter, clatter, giggle, squeeze;
Movies, motors, neck, knees.
Fags, fuss. "There's Charlie. Oo!
See you later. Tooraloo!"

2. A POLITICIAN

"No, sir, I did not seek to run."
Vast importance; humor, none.
Alluring voice, uncertain clothes,
Jovial pre-election pose:
"A charming child. How's Mrs Smith?"
Blarney, bombast, bogey, myth.
"Watch Jones; he's got a good strong team.
The party, sir, must be supreme!"
Inside knowledge, strings, ropes,
Office!! Tactics, fears, hopes.
"I rise to — Mr Speaker, sir!
I did not say it. I aver
I said I — What? Where are my notes?"
Votes, votes, votes, votes.
Deserted? Me? It's quite absurd.
You read the context, word for word.
'Twas they left me. A rotten game!
My principles remain the same."

3. AN ELECTRIC TRAM

Crush, jostle, push, battle,
  Crash, rumble, clang!
Noise, noise, rattle, rattle,
  Boom, thunder, clang!
Shoulders, elbows, parcels, knees,
Clash, rumble. "Twopence, please."

WALKING IN THE RAIN

WALKING on a Melbourne night, walking in the rain —
Red lights, green lights in an ebon sea —
We are back with Oberon in fairyland again —
Car lights flashing in a whirling fantasy.
Wet stones shimmering, a merry, magic town;
White lights glimmering and dancing, dancing down;
Street bells, sweet bells ringing a refrain —
Walking on a Melbourne night, walking in the rain.

Walking on a wet night thro' a shining town —
Swift feet, light feet tapping to and fro —
Silver on the plane trees, silver falling down
To a silver river where the fairy coaches go.
Soft rain pattering adown the elfin way,
Sly winds scattering the leaves of yesterday.
Who would fall to muttering at Winter's kindly frown,
Walking on a wet night thro' a shining town?

Walking on a Melbourne night, walking in the rain —
Hoarse coughs, hard coughs, wheezy coughs and loud —
Oh, the dread catarrhal curse! Oh, the bronchial bane!
Grim forms, soaked forms hasting thro' the crowd,
Wet feet squishing with a sad and sodden tread,
Wet folk wishing they were safe at home in bed.
Ack — Ack — Ishing! Gosh! I've got the 'flu agaid!
Walkig on a Belbud dight, walkig id the raid.

THE FAIRY POLICEMAN

Two small children — brother and sister — were found roaming unattended in the thick of the city traffic yesterday. They were taken to Russell Street, where the sergeant in charge told them fairy tales until their mother claimed them.

OH, he was big an' tall an' fierce
With two great eyes that seemed to pierce
You froo an' froo; an' when he spoke
He rumbled, like if echoes woke
In some big ogre's cave. His feet
Were big as that! — to walk his beat.
An' when he talked we were afraid
Of all the 'normous noise he made.

His face was big an' broad an' red
A shiny helmet on his head
Made him so tall. An' he was dressed
Wif shiny buttons down his chest.
We trembled when he stooped and took
Both ours in his big hand — we shook.
But when he smiled! — Why! You could see
He was as nice as nice could be.

An' then he sat an' told us — true—
Not stories that would frighten you,
Of putting bad men into gaols
But — you can't guess it — fairy tales!
Yes, funny things to make you laugh
About a funny ole giraffe,
'N bears 'n' crockendiles an' fings
An' little piggieswhat had wings.

I fink he was a fairy p'leece,
The sort of one 'at keeps the peace
Where people have a jolly time—
Most likely in a pantomime.
An' now, with Christmas coming near,
I wouldn't be surprised to hear
He 'tends to all the traffic laws
For his big brother, Santa Claus.

I used to fink one time, I did,
When I was just a little kid,
'At p'leecemen were big savage men
'At frightened little fellers when
They frew a stone or ran away
Unnoticed in the street to play.
But now, when I grow to a man,
I'll be a p'leeceman if I can.

CONCERNING SWEEPERS

Again this week, the City Council chose the windiest day to scatter sand on St. Kilda road, and the sweepers, human and mechanical, were out in force.

The other day I walked abroad,
While fierce winds howled and leapt;
And lo! I came upon a man
Who swept, and swept, and swept.

Along the street he swept the dust —
Stray refuse. But, alack!
Each time a broom-full forth he thrust,
The mad winds swept it back.

And still he swept, tho' naught he gleaned —
A patient man was he.
To me his wild endeavor seemed
But sheer futility.

"Good fellow," I exclaimed, "why sweep,
And sweep, and sweep again,
While teasing gales that howl and leap
Make all your sweeping vain?"

The surly fellow answered, "Keep
Your block! What's that to you?
I sweep because I have to sweep;
The Council pays me to."

Just then a gust caught up his heap,
And sent it swirling high.
"See that! What profits it to sweep
On such a day?" said I.

"Your task is hopeless, man!" I cried.
I argued, pleaded wept!
But he, poor fellow, turned aside
And swept,
And swept,
And swept.

A LAY OF OLDEN LAYERS

Egg-laying competitions are again becoming very popular, and published scores seem to indicate close and exciting contests.

"THEM was the days!" said the old sport, Ben —
  Them old egg-layin' days,
When a egg was a egg an' a 'en was a 'en;
  "Till we fell for the gam'lin' craze.
But we bred reel birds an' we risked our tin,
  An' we cheered 'em on like mad
Till it got too 'ot, an' the crooks got in,
  An' a noble sport went bad.

"Me? I was lucky. Me last big race
  Was the time — 'fore you were born —
When I put me shirt for a win or place
  On Meg, me white Leg'orn.
Excitement? Man! It was win or bust,
  But I got fair odds on Meg,
A sprintin' bird as a man could trust,
  An', lad, she knoo 'er egg.

"They're off! . . . A Langshang took the lead,
  An' Meg was lyin' third.
To them as didn't know 'er breed
  She looked a beaten bird.
But I knoo my 'en an' I knoo the game
  An' I knoo wot pace she 'ad.
Then, egg an' egg, to the turn they came;
  An' the crowd went yellin' mad.

"'She wins! She don't! The Langshang's done!'
  Then me good old stayer, Meg,
She come in the straight with 'er famous run
  An' won be arf a egg."

FLAPPER FANTASIA

A newspaper correspondent complains that, while the modern young miss is more or less decorative in an artificial way, her fund of intelligent conversation and her vocabulary leave much to be desired.

I SAW them meet upon a crowded tram.
First, they stood beak to beak as pigeons do;
Then gushing floods of speech burst every dam:
"Dawling!" "Mai dawling! Is it REALLY you?"
Their finger-nails were painted signal-red,
Their lips bright mauve, their noses white as starch,
A scrap of straw absurdly decked each head,
Their brows were plucked down to a slender arch.

"DAWLING!" "But, DAWLING! Fency meeting HERE!
Of ALL the places in this fraightful town!"
"Why, yes. It's ebsolutely THRILLING, dear!"
"It's AGES since I saw you! DO sit down!"
"What's new? Why, DAWLING, what a gorgeous DRESS!"
"THIS rag?" "But, DEAR! It's gorgeously DIVAIN!"
"Not REALLY, sweet?" "But definitely, YES!
It mekes me feel a perfect FRUMP in main."
"But LISTEN, dawling (whisper) Hev you heard?"
"Not GEORGE? Mai DEAR! How utterly EBSURD!"

ROUND one. They went to corners for repair;
Re-powdered noses and repainted lips,
Touched here and there their strangely plastic hair
Deftly and cunningly with finger-tips,
Gazing in mirrors raptly as they toiled;
Then sat, both strangely vague and listless eyed,
Until one more idea within them boiled,
And once again the flood-gates opened wide:

"DAWLING!" "But, sweet, it's mejic'ly DIVAIN
Thet we should meet when AGES hev gone bai" —
"But, sweetness, Ai em LIVING on this lain —
Hev done for YEARS." "But, PRECIOUS! So hev AI!"
"But, dawling, NO!" "But, dawling, YES, Ai say!"
"DAWLING! How weird we hev not MET before!" . . .
So they ran on, intensely, to display
Their vast vocabularies o'er and o'er.
Deep in the news I hid my burning face,
And gloatingly perused a murder case.

THE TWO BEES — AN ALLEGORY

The present unprecedented succession of frosty nights and clear, sunny days seems greatly to have mystified the bee nation. In sunlit gardens, devoid of flowers, bees sit idly about on twigs and fences, wearing an air of utter bewilderment. An occasional butterfly is also seen.

HANGING about with their hands in their pockets,
  Sitting around in the sun,
A couple of bees were taking their ease
  This morn when the day had begun.
And they looked forlorn on this sunlit morn,
  In my garden, ravished of flowers,
So, "Pardon," said I. "Will you tell me why
  You idle away the hours?"
And one sat — HERE,
  And the other sat — THERE,
And regarded the world with a mystified stare.

With a listless expression, "It's just the depression,"
  The first bee said, with a sob,
"Did you ever," said he, "see an idle bee
  When a bee had a chance of a job?
We are here because economical laws
  Seem very upset indeed,
And the job is denied." But the second bee cried,
  "Oh, please, sir! Spare us a feed!"
And one sat — HERE,
  And the other sat — THERE,
And begged for a meal, if I'd one to spare.

"It may seem to you strange that a bee should be begging,"
  Hastily said bee two;
"But with nights a-freeze and such days as these,
  Well, what is a bee to do?
For there's never a sup — But I cried, "Cheer up!"
  And I went to the house and got,
From the larder's hoard, where the sweets are stored,
  Some honey we kept in a pot.
And as one sat — HERE,
  And the other sat — THERE,
I left them alone, each to gobble his share.

I, being inquisitive, went to revisit
Those bees I had made so glad.
They were both stone dead! Most messily spread
In the honey. I felt quite sad.
But a flash butterfly, who was fluttering by,
Seemed curiously annoyed.
"It"s outrageous!" she said, with a toss of her head.
"That's the worst of these unemployed."
But one lay — HERE,
And the other lay — THERE,
And both seemed utterly shorn of care.

PREJUDICE

Yesterday a prisoner, on being asked why he ran away when being taken to prison, replied, "I never liked the place."

SOME'OW I never liked the place.
I couldn't tell you why.
They gives their guest fair food an' rest,
And the tariff isn't high,
And they're most attentive night an' day,
Whenever you go there to stay.

Their invites is so pressing like;
The host, 'e loves you so
That when they've got you on the spot,
They 'ates to let you go.
An' yet, I've always noticed when
You leave they don't say, "Come again."

Yet, some day, when I least expect,
An' ain't inclined to go,
One of their cops in on me drops,
An' simply won't take "No."
An', at sich times, it don't seem nice
To let 'em see your prejudice.

A bloke 'as other things to do,
An' other spots to go.
If they'd agree to let me be,
An' wouldn't press me so,
Then gladly, if they didn't mind,
I'd go there when I felt inclined.

THE GNU

In exchange for two kangaroos the Zoological Gardens will soon receive two South African white-tailed gnus.

I haven't been down to the Zoo—
Have you? —
For more than a year or two
To view
The animals there — of the Polar bear
Or the puma I hadn't seen hide or hair
For many a day.
And I must say
The pigeons and parrots with plumage gay
Seemed ages and ages and ages away.

For I thought, as a man will do,
I knew
Them all, from the kangaroo
Right through
To the whatshisname. And to see the same
Old animals seemed a trifle tame.
For I'd seen the lot —
Both the hippopot —
Amus and the thingamy — You know what.

However, I'd nothing to do
A few
Days since; so I went to view
The Zoo;
And an animal there seemed somewhat rare,
So I said to a keeper standing there —
A keeper who
Had nothing to do
But answer the silly remarks of the few,
Prize idiots like, say, me — and you.

I said to the man in blue,
"It's true,"
I said, "That I one time knew
A few
Of the animals here; but this seems queer.
When did a thing like that appear?"
But the man said "Who
In the world are you?
Why the thing's been here for a week or two."
So I knew 'twas a gnu, and a new gnu too.

HEREDITY

A French professor of agriculture has discovered that a ration of wine is good for hens. After experimenting he declares that wet hens lay more eggs than teetotal ones.

YOU may ask me (said the rooster)
Why I wander in a haze
In the way no rooster useter
In the old teetotal days.

You may ask me why I wobble
With a queer uncertain walk,
And incontinently gobble
At a hiccup when I talk.

Yet I'm all for prohibition,
And my case is most forlorn,
For this terrible condition
Came about when I was born.

And the reason that I tip so
On my strange uncertain legs
Is that mother was a dipso
And laid alcoholic eggs.

THE THIEF

"Boarders Must Breathe," declares a headline, referring to the Health Commission's draft regulations recently submitted to the municipalities.

The landlord sat by the kitchen fire
  Where the porridge pot was seething;
And he said to his wife, "Joy of my life,
  I hear a boarder breathing!"

And she cried, "How dare he steal our air?
  It's just what I expected!
He has his bed and he's been well fed!
  This wretch I've long suspected!

"I saw last night that his eyes were bright,
  As if with respiration,
And the night before I heard him snore,
  This needs some explanation!"

They tip-toed soft to the dingy loft
  Where the boarder still was lying.
They listened there on the crazy stair
  And they plainly heard him sighing.

With an ugly sneer: "Our atmosphere,"
  The landlord cried, "You're stealing!
Our children's air that we ill can spare.
  Wretch! Do you lack all feeling?"

With savage wrath they cast him forth,
  As he yelled in desperation.
But he quickly died of the air supplied
  By the City Corporation.

CORROBORATION

The Anglican Archbishop of Perth, Dr. Riley, says that certain anonymous letter-writers expressed the wish that he should go to hell and hear the shrieks of the damned, because he would not support Prohibition.

1. And, lo, it came to pass that the Archbishop, in a dream, decended
2. Into hell. Throwing a sop to Cerberus — a sop soaked in the wine of the country — he managed to

3. Pass the portals; for the heart of Cerberus was made glad and all his three heads were swimming in

4. Different directions. And, standing just within the gates, the good Archbishop listened unto the shrieks of the

5. Damned. And, behold, they shrieked in divers tongues — some in Sanscrit, some in Chaldean, some in Coptic roots, many in the Teuton tongue, and some few in the dinkum

6. Aussie lingo. And it was so. Then, being something of a linguist and a scholar, the good Archbishop set down notes in shorthand upon his

7. Asbestos tablet; taking them verbatim (even those that were verboten) in the Teuton tongue, and the Aussie tongue; aye, even in the Coptic root and in the language of the Northern American who shrieked lustily through the flames and

8. His nose; for, "Behold," he shrieked, "this is even worse than America. For in hell there are no bootleggers!" And, lo, the heart of the good Archbishop was sore within him for

9. He had foreseen this thing and

10. He went on taking notes upon his tablet of

11. Asbestos; while Cerberus yet slept, with his three heads pillowed peacefully upon three separate blocks of

12. Brimstone. And, behold, the good Archbishop after a space, awoke again upon

13. Earth, and faced his accusers, saying unto them, "I

14. Told you so." And they replied "What's

15. Doing? Are you not now a Prohibitionist?" And he answered them, saying, "Not on

16. Your life. I have beheld the only Prohibitionist country in the

17. Universe, and my heart is sad; for I have heard the nations shriek in divers tongues and, one and all, the shriek for

18. Drinks —

19. For the strong drink, for the one half of one per cent. drink, aye, even for the weak drink down unto the lemon squash and the cocoa that destroyeth. And I will NOT support your Prohibition for it maketh the nations to shriek." And the good

20. Archbishop went his way, smiling. For he knew that he had done good work; for down in

21. Hell the good and wise dog, Cerberus, having tasted of the joy of life has become a

22. Bootlegger.

DOOLEY

In rain and mud, despite the protests of officials, Mr Dooley, the New South Wales Speaker, held up the Duke's car near Katoomba, and persuaded the Duke and Duchess to inspect the Anzac Memorial Hospital.

Who barred the progress of a Duke?
Dooley! — Dooley!
And handed Brass-hats stern rebuke —
Dooley! — Dooley!
Injustice fired his Celtic blood;
He stopped the motor in the mud,
And proved Officialdom a dud.
Whiroo! — Dooley!

The Duke he stared, the Duke he frowned —
Dooley! — Dooley.
Despite the stare, despite the frown
Of that stern scion of the Crown,
They couldn't throw a good man down.
Whiroo! — Dooley!

Surprised officials stood aghast —
Dooley! — Dooley!
And sought with savage looks to blast
Dooley! — Dooley!
But tho' with threats they clustered round,
And tho' the Duke still stared and frowned,
The interloper stood his ground.
Whiroo! — Dooley!

Who is it has the wheedling tone?
Dooley! — Dooley!
Who is it's kissed the blarney stone?
Dooley! — Dooley!
With pleasant words, meant to beguile
He sought the Duchess with a smile
And spoke with her the briefest while.
Whiroo! — Dooley!

The Duchess smiled as well she can —
Dooley! — Dooley!
Says she, "He is a charmin' man" —
Dooley! — Dooley!
She nudged the Duke, and not in vain;
He lost his frown and smiled again,
And both got out into the rain.
Whiroo! — Dooley!

Officials spluttered in despair —
Dooley! — Dooley!
But off he took the Royal pair —
Dooley! — Dooley!
He triumphed then, say what you may;
And Mishter Dooley won the day.
Faugh-a-ballagh! Clear the way!
Whiroo! — Dooley!

DITTIES OF DEBUNK

THE OPERATION

OH, come in, dear; and thank you for the flowers.
They do so cheer one, tending to repine
While lying here like this for hours and hours
After an operation such as mine.
What? Serious? My pet! Have you not heard?
I thought that all my friends — Come closer, dear.
Of course the doctor wouldn't say a word;
But — (Whisper, whisper, whisper). Yes; thro' here.

Well. Been to any shows? . . . I've heard that's good.
I shan't see one for weeks and weeks, I fear.
Yes; rest's the only thing. I really should
Go right away. My operation, dear —
Almost unique. And complicated? Sweet!
The doctor says he marvels how I bore
So much. Why, it's the talk of Collins Street.
And — (Whisper, whisper, whisper). Yes; and more!

Bridge? Oh, at Maud de Grubb's. Now there's a cat.
The way she talked you'd think she'd been half slain;
And hers a mild appendix case at that!
She'll never try to talk me down again.
And Sonia's silly tonsils. Why, I laugh
When I think how I used to squirm with dread
To hear them; thinking them near cut in half;
But — (Whisper, whisper, whisper) — doctor said.

Oh, must you go? Well, do come soon again.
I have such lots and lots I want to tell —
Such gorgeous details that I must explain,
Such heaps and heaps to talk of when I'm well.
Why — (Whisper, whisper, whisper). Ghastly? Yes!
And — (Whisper, whisper, whisper) — simply gnawed,
And — (Whisper, whisper, whisper). Such distress!
Dear, do come soon. Bring Sonia and Maud.

MRS DOOZENBERRY

HEAVENS! There's the door-bell! Peep around the window-shade.
Who is it, Arthur dear? Oh, not THAT!
Not Mrs DOOZENBERRY-old MOTHER DOOZENBERRY?
  I KNOW she's your director's wife — the dull old cat!
But . . . Why — Mrs Doozenberry! DEAR Mrs Doozenberry,
  Just this VERY moment we were gossiping of you.
I said, "It must be ages since we saw Mrs Doozenberry.
  I do HOPE she isn't ailing." Sit in THIS chair, do.

Tea, Mrs Doozenberry? Just a cup of China tea.
  Truly GRIEVED am I to hear of your poor health,
And I QUITE agree with all you say, Mrs Doozenberry:
  If the body's ailing what's the USE of wordly wealth?
Others, Mrs Doozenberry — DEAR Mrs Doozenberry —
  Helping others on their way . . . I QUITE see what you mean.
But you always WERE so thoughtful tho' — so very, VERY charitable.
  (Why, she's rolling in it, and she doesn't spend a bean).

SHAWLS, Mrs Doozenberry? Missionary enterprise?
  For women of Manchuria — AND mufflers for the neck?
DEAR Mrs Doozenberry! How they MUST depend on you.
  DO have another cake while Arthur writes a cheque.
I've READ about Manchuria. Oh? Quite a NEW Society?
  And they've made you President? But of COURSE they would,
DEAR Mrs Doozenberry. Who could be so CAPABLE?
  So LIKE you, Mrs Doozenberry — always doing good.

Do you REALLY have to go, dear Mrs Doozenberry?
  Thanks SO much for calling, and this most uplifting chat.
Goodbai. Come again. Goodbai, Mrs Doozenberry . . .
  WHAT a woman! What a vampire! I am absolutely flat!
Oh, I KNOW she's a director's wife. But never tell me, Arthur dear,
  I do not help you earn a crust. I've earned a martyr's crown!
Half an hour of agony! That awful Mrs Doozenberry!
  What's the least you had to give her? That's another guinea down.

FEED THE BRUTE

OH, MERCY! Is it five o'clock? Why, hello, Arthur, dear.
Just on time. The rubber's finished. And I've lost again, I fear.
What am I owing Gertrude? Fifteen shillings? 'Fraid it's so.
That's two pounds ten I'm down this week; and two more days to go.
Oh, please don't fidget, Arthur! We'll be home with hours to spare.
If you can't keep the car a while, lend me a taxi fare.
What have we got for dinner? How like a man. Dear me!
It's your favorite, Arthur, darling. You'll see.

Will you be at Maud's on Friday, Grace? Yes, dear, it's rather far.
What can poor women do whose men won't buy a second car?
Arthur says we can't afford it. Isn't that just like a man?
If he'll cut his club expenses, I am almost sure we can.
Oh, we keep economising. But there's bridge and golf and shows.
My own housekeeping money goes like water, Heaven knows.
Oh, Arthur! Don't be greedy! Dinner won't be very late.
It's your favorite, Arthur darling! You wait.

Thanks so much, Gertrude dearest, for the lovely afternoon.
My place next week. I must win back some of my losses soon.
Where was it, Grace, you told me that you saw that stunning hat?
Only five guineas! Arthur, dear, you'll have to buy me that.
Oh, please forget your dinner. There's no need to throw a fit.
You've had your lunch; and I'm quite sure I couldn't eat a bit.
And I've only nibbled savories, and chocolate, and cake.
You'll have your favorite at home. All ready in a shake.

Oh, those savories, dear Gertrude. What delicious things they are.
I'll just jot down the recipe. Arthur, you start the car.
Olives, you say? . . . Oh, drat the man! What ails my husband now
Outside there? He can't start it? Heavens! What a shocking row!
He always lets the thing get cold when I am in a rush.
'Fraid I must fly. Goodbye, dears . . . Arthur! Please! Such language! Hush!
No need to lose your temper. I'll soon have the table spread.
Your dinner/ I keep telling you. Your favorite. Fried bread.

DIPLOMACY

I DON'T think I'd do it, Mrs Pendlebury-Rockingham.
I don't think I'd do it, altogether, Miss Millane.
As the head of this Committee
I do think 'twould be a pity
If our action were precipitate; I think we should refrain.
Mrs Dowser, don't you think —
Miss Bellwether, Mrs Blink —
That, ere seeking his subscription, we should pause a while and think?
Major Moppup may be marvellous, an absolute old dear;
But don't you think to call on him so early might seem — queer?
He has just come to the district, and we none of us know much —
Saving what we learn from rumors. Is his money fit to touch?
His possessions may be great,
But I think it wise to wait.
Don't you feel it, Mrs Dagglethorp? O, quaite, quaite, quaite.

I don't think I'd venture, Mrs Pendlebury-Rockingham.
No, I don't think I'd venture just at present, Miss Millane.
I've explained, with perfect clarity,
Ours is a worthy charity.
The sources of its income must be quite without a stain.
Mrs Mumble, will you move?
Mrs Dimm, do you approve?
Will you second that we shelve it till we definitely prove
Major Moppup is a gentleman beyond the least reproach?
Then the question of his contribution later we can broach.
(Why, he's just the match for Mabel, and he's simply soused in pelf!
Do the cats think they can call on him before I call myself?)
All in favor? May I state
It is wiser far to wait —
Moved, seconded, and — carried, ladies! Quaite, quaite, quaite.

CULCHER AND LINGO

A FREE VERSE REVIEW

I love writing free verse because it
Is so easy.
You don't have to rhyme or
Trouble about metre.
It is just prose sawn up into
Unequal lengths. A lot of
People who write it are very
Proud of their efforts; but I am
Not. However, let
Us see what we can do
With a little review.
(That's all wrong, because it rhymes; but that's a habit not easily overcome, and we make up for it by being a little more erratic than usual concerning the length of the Lines.)
Now, let us see what is doing in the world. It is said that Federal
Expenditure
Is a great deal over the odds, and a number of people are shouting loudly for
Economy, which they may get — perhaps —
Perhaps not. De Valera has gone to
Cork,
Probably with the idea of keeping
Afloat;
But even Cork is unlikely to save him from sinking. The French
President has been shot at and
Missed; and a Pentridge prisoner has done a dash successfully; and
Girls with low necks weer given the bird by a
Cardinal in Rome, who
Gave it to them in the neck because
The necks were low; and
Aeroplanes are off the Scottish coast looking for
Herrings, which seems to be rather a fishy thing for
Aeroplanes to do. However, Germany
Paid up on Saturday, after trying

To drag a lot of herrings across
The trail, which possibly accounts for the aeroplanes'
Search. A Melbourne pawnbroker lost £3000; and the Federal
Treasurer is busy preparing his
Budget; and some of the shearers are
Shearing, while some are
Not.
I'm a little bit tired of this free verse
Because the further you go the worse
You fare.
So there!
It's just mere prose chopped up in bits,
And none of it rhymes and none of it fits.
It's bosh,
By gosh!
But since it's written, well, let it go,
For the writing of rhyme is rather slow.
But, nevertheless,
I must confess
I love writing free
Verse, because it
Is so
Easy.

LINGO

A correspondent in a morning paper complains bitterly of the "indescribable intonation" taught to children in some schools, and quotes a verse of Tennyson, as taught, to illustrate his grievance.

As Tennyson wrote it:

Ring out, wild bells, to the wild sky,
  The flying cloud, the frosty light.
  The year is dying in the night;
Ring out, wild bells, and let him die.

As the correspondent says it is taught in schools:

Ring ote, waild bells, to the waild skaye,
  The flaying clode, the frosty laight.
  The yeah is daying in the naight.
Ring ote, waild bells, and let him daye.

The Dinkum Aussie of it:

Ring eout, woild bells, to the woild skoy,
  The floyin' cleoud, the frosty loight,
  The year is doyin' in the noight.
Ring eout, woild bells, an' let 'im doy.

BOWYANG'S GRAND OPERA

Glamor and Romance

Melbun
Septemer 19

deer frend

me an bill smith was to tierd to go to the show a saterdy after our long ike but our kind frend that we are stoppin with in albert park took us to the oprer on saterdy nite

an i tell you strait i never seen nuthink so excitin in me life

i thort ole bills eyes wud drop out of is ed

tork about them merikin gangster fillums

they was sunday skool picknick cumpared to them 2 blud thursty oprers we seen

ther was 2 of em one called sumpthink like rustick anna an the uther pally archie

but taik it from me archie wasent nun to pally wen it cum to the nife stickin

i never see sich a pritty bit of stickin since ole jim airey killed is 6 pigs in one day the time bakin was on the up me onley trubbel was all that singing bein in a furrin tung

i ad to keep arskin the bloke nex me wot thay was sayin

but e seamed a pritty igerint sorter cove that dident no latin eether an bime bi e got quite disagreeble

well i rekun if them furrin oprers goes so well we ad ort to ave a orstralyun gran oprer as wud go twice as well

avin nuthink to do of a sundy i maid up a bit of a plot meself outer me own ed and if you appen to no a bloke wot is andy with choons e cud sling in a bit of musick an we got a shure winner

as follers erewith i give a bit of a short sinopis of me grate plot fer orstralyun gran oprer

the ero wich is a tenner is a yung country feller wot as gon to town an got a job in a abators stickin cattil

is naim is antonio wallibi an the furst seen is a big cattil stickin corus with plenty of blud and the ero is stickin em reel good an is out to brake the slortermens rekkud wen orl of a suddin as e is abowt to plung is gory blade inter the neck of a red an wite poley effer e discuvvers she is nun other than is pet carf strorbery wot e plaid with on is fathers farm wen e was a innercint child

e is art broke by the pleadin look in the effers eye an just as e slings is nife away in discust oo shud cum on the seen but lino sirsingle the drovers pritty dorter from gipsland

thay falls in luv at fust site an in a verry pritty jewett she irges im to call a slortermens strike an demand the umain killin of bullicks by given em cloraform befor deth

ther then cums on the seen the villin of the peece a olesail buchers son be the naim of marco undercut a bloke with a barytone voyce greesy air an a durty look

undercut trys to intise lino away frum antonio by offerin to teech er the trick of wayin yer and with a pound of stake but antonio its im with a pluck an the curtin falls on ack one

in ack 2 the big slortermens strike is on

"i thort ole Bills eyes wud drop out of is ed."

the slortermen ave downed everythink excep ther nifes wich they is flashin at a butey corus of olesail buchers wot is drest like a balit an does a verry pritty dance intitled the wing-rib one step

billo brisket one of the strikers is owever a low ound in leeg with undercut and elps im obduck lino to is manshin in toorack but after a big fite she is reskewed by antonio wallibi with the elp of is busum frend a pertater digger frum gunns gully by the naim of apolo fosfate

this ere apolo is a shrood ed an e perswades antonio to buy a lot of pertater land wile the markit is cheep

this ack closes with antonio an apolo cuttin braken on their noo farm wile lino sersingle playin a akorjin sittin on the fence

in ack 3 the strike is still on an marco undercut trine to brake it by doin all the killin in is fathers yard

bein out of practis e stabs imself in mistake for a cow an falls ded

apolo fosfate persuades all the slortermen to becum vegetarians an force all the rest of the country to eat nuthink but pertaters an greens.

antonio and apolo maiks ther forchins outer spuds wich as gon to 50 quid a tun antonio marrys lino and all live appy ever after.

curtin

now if that oprer dont nock em silly wen it is put on you can call be bad juge and a muttin eded mutt

hopin you are the saim

Yores truly

BEN BOWYANG.

PS If it is on wile we are down me and bil is goin to see that grate murder case oprer riggy letto or the body in the bag.

wud you like to cum B.B.

AN INVITATION TO SONG

The Young Bolshevik Party of Russia has opened a campaign to abolish grammar. They hold that grammar rules deaden every creative effort among the young.

ERE'S noos! 'Ere's 'ope! 'Ere's joy for poits, dumb
Thro' weary years, becos, when songs 'ave come
They died unsung, 'cos them grammatic rools
Gagged minstrelsy; an' the loud laugh of fools
Done genius in, while muses, fair but frail
'Cos of their accent, was beyond the pale.

Oh, them proud songs that 'ad no chance to live
Becos the verb don't fit the nom'native!
Oh, them sweet bards, with fancy flowin' free,
'Oo's genders, moods an' tenses don't agree!
An' so their muses, with the 'arp strings bust,
'Ave got to take in washin' for a crust.

I've sung rare things, I 'ave, of life an' love,
Fit for the 'earin' of the gawds above;
To see the dilly tanties cut up rough
An' call my efferts rood, unculcher'd stuff.
Culcher? The blighters dunno where to look.
Culcher ain't prisoned in a grammar book.

Look 'ere. A rose by any other name,
As Shakespeare tells a bloke, would smell the same.
An' Shakespeare knoo. He never stopped to turn
The dictionary over for to learn
The meanin' of a word; but in it went;
An' mugs were left to find out wot 'e meant.

I've 'eard a grey thrush pipin' in a tree,
'E never stopped to think the verb to be
Should take the same case after as before.
'E sung. 'E poured out all the thrush's lore
Fearless an' flutin' free; an' never give
A dam about the split infinitive.

So, blokes, 'ere's 'ope! Choon up yer lyres with me,
An' so pour out yer souls in verse that free —
Not free from rhyme or rhythm, but the rools
That some schoolmaster made to govern fools.
Sing 'igh, you coots! Chuck grammar to the dogs!
Embrace yer muse, an' snout the pedagogues!

MY SCENARIO

Amongst other prizes, the Commonwealth Government is offering two of £500 each for film scenarios.

OH, I've got a lovely story that I've thought out all myself;
 It will make a gorgeous picture, I am sure.
(Mind, it isn't for the money, for I am not keen on pelf,
 And my attitude to Art is very pure).
It is full of real heart-int'rest, mother-love and passion rare,
 And gun-fights and a bad, bold man (who dies),
And a big, strong he-man hero with divinely marcelled hair;
 And I really think it ought to win the prize.

The hero falls on evil days and sinks and sinks quite low
 (This is where the villain comes upon the scene),
But the mother writes a letter pointing out the way to go
 (We will show the letter, close-up, on the screen);
Then Augustus (that's the hero) meets a lovely girl by chance
 With great, big, soulful, golf-ball, baby eyes,
And undying love comes to them at the very first brief glance.
 Oh, I really think it ought to win the prize.

But ways of true love ne'er run smooth, and lots of dreadful things
 Occur, and all their plans turn out amiss.
But thro' the fights and flights and frights she clings and clings and clings
 To win him with the last, long, luscious kiss.
I don't know much of writing things — scenarios and such;
 Still, one never really knows what one can do.
But the theme is so original and has so quaint a touch,
 That I think it ought to win the prize. Don't you?

CULTURE ON THE FARM

The periodic criticism of the allegedly "awful Australian accent" has again burst forth recently among somewhat one-eyed pedants who, while revering strange dialects hallowed by age and custom in older lands, affect to abominate dialects of recent vintage. The radio, however, is said to be doing something to correct our "slovenly pronunciation," particularly in the remoter districts.

ERE'S wireless workin' wonders on the farmland,
Culcher's spreadin' thro' the cowyard like a fire —
(As you were.) It's "cultuah" reely.
Gotter mouth it kinder mealy.
An' our edja — ed-youcation's climbin' higher.
Ai mean to say, ouah accent's quaite too quaite.
Stone ther crows! Ouah progress nothin' now can bork.
An' we're thankful for these mercies,
Since the prattle of the Percys
Fills the ether, for to teach us 'ow ter tork.

Why, we might 'ave — h-h-have the Oxford Collidge 'andy
Right in the old 'ome paddick by our door,
Once, in accents loose and draggly
We referred to Pag-lee-aggly;
Now we calls it Par-lee-archie evermore.
An' we misnamed poor old Strorb'ry somethin' awful.
An' 'ow? — That is, Ai means to say, "And hah-oo?"
But we've recent come to see 'ow
We been wrong to call 'er kee-ow;
An' we always calls 'er cah-oo, nah-oo.

I owns we gits confused upon occasions
When the crooners an' the jazz is comin' threw,
With the old 'Ill-Billies whoopin',
An' that ritzy oopah-doopin':
"'Wa'g'g'e'r'n 'w'eels." Sez me. "Okay. I'm tellin' yew."
In ouah perfect aisolation from Ort centres
Even English sorta gits our goat a bit
When gives a "talk" to wind yah
With their "Pom-trees ovah Ind-yah," Then, "Sa-am, Sa-am,
Pick oop tha Mooskit" don't quite fit.

So the cow-'ands an' the plough-
'ands gits fair puzzled,
  But they waits till little Willie
calls the card,
With 'is Stock Exchange
advaises,
An' the latest Fat Stock Praices.
  Then they knows they're 'ome
an' dried, an' studies 'ard.

An' ole Storb'ry comes an'
listens at the doorway;
  An', spare me days! She's
gittin' reel 'igh-brah-oo.
For she never sez "Mee-oo!"
Like the way she useter do;
  Not 'er. She bellers "Mah-oo!"
nah-oo!

NUTHINOO

According to a recent cable, Dr. Vizetelly, the American texicographer, calls special attention to the protogram, and to what he considers is a modern tendency to use telescopic language, such as: "Statofoon," meaning, "Staying late at the office this afternoon". But a modified form of this has been employed in Australia for a long time.

ARFAMO! Arfamo!
Snuthin nooin this yahno.
Tasaytha telescopic word
Is nooan novel is absurd.
Cozwy? Inoa certin bloke,
A palamine, oos nevaspoke
In anyuther wayfer years.
Itaintso nooaz it appears.

Supposya meetim inna street:
"Owdoo," sezee. "I oped ide meet
A chapat adda boberto,
Cozime as dryasdust. Ainchoo?
Wahsaywe dodgin ovareer?
They gotta decent branabeer."
Anso, ocorse, we duzzaduck,
An I sez, "Selth." An eesez,
"Sluck."

"I dunno wya work," sezee.
"Work aina bitta goota me.
Yawanna getta decent lurk
Like me, an wudenavta work.
I never failta scora feed,
Or drink, or anythinineed;
So I dunavta keepajob.
Say, avyagotta nutherbob?"

So, azzi sezza wilago,
Ther's nuthin nooin this yahno.
Coz telescopic words this way
Comes sorta natchril yumasay.
Ferever since the ages dim
We've spokum regler,
meeanim '. . .
Still, azzi aingot plennipelf,
I wisheed goan loosiself.

BALLADE OF CAPTIOUS CRITICS

In a satire recently broadcast an Australian writer charged Australia's more erudite critics with condemning the work of Australians merely because it is Australian. Critics of similar mental habit have before now condemned England's present Laureate for breaking new poetic ground.

STUFFED with tradition and trammels of yore,
Cramped in their studies, they sneer and scold
At the strange, new passions young hearts would pour
  Thro' a sunlit land, and a tale unfold
  Of youth's ambition — new-minted gold
Fresh from life's furnace, all aglow —
  With none of its worth are their hearts cajoled,
If it waken no echo of things they know.

Their minds close cluttered with olden lore,
  Their praise for the new is charily doled;
Their memories, clogged with a moss-grown store
  Of dead men's wisdom, naught else may hold
  The flight of an eaglet, overbold,
Is an impudent thing, as their judgments go;
  And the song of a bush bird leaves them cold,
If it waken no echo of things they know.

Songs that have sprung from this virgin shore,
  Tales that are turned from an unworn mould,
These be but follies that grieve them sore —
  Rhymes the old troubadours have not trolled.
  Themes must be borrowed from arts of old;
For originality irks them so,
  And the voice of the bush must be controlled,
If it waken no echo of things they know.

AUTUMN OBSEQUIES

RIPE Autumn is a lovely time for purposes of facile rhyme that trippingly come to the pen to gladden hearts of writing men; and so I haste, before it goes, to raise this slab of rhyming prose: a stone for Autumn, dying Autumn, when, because the mood has caught 'em, bards, like birds, tho' scant of words, needs must sing as nature taught 'em.

SINCE Autumn lingers late this year time yet remains for stating here how bards insist that Autumn "grieves" because it rhymes so well with "leaves"; and likewise with the "warm, wet breeze" that gently stirs the "painted trees" in Autumn, Autumn, lovely Autumn, glowing where the sun has caught 'em. Let us then, oh, rhyming men, hold this laggard last post-mortem.

IN such a mood it seems to me a man is very like a tree, casting off as summer dies the garb of gaudy butterflies; yet not, like trees, to winter grim presenting an unsheltered limb; but, wrapping further foliage about them, men fear Winter's rage when Autumn, Autumn, trait'rous Autumn, blowing hot and cold, has brought 'em qualms and chills and various ills that give 'em toko when they've caught 'em.

AUTUMN farewell, farewell, farewell! This repetition suits me well. Crook rhyming, but, in point of fact, it keeps the rhythmic beat intact; and, tho' this song's a silly thing, you must admit it has a swing. Oh, Autumn, Autumn, niggard Autumn! (Rhymes are rarer than I'd thought 'em). The last bird grieves. Sweep up the leaves. Farewell! Goo' bye! Hic facet Autumn.

TWO GENTLEMEN OF FOOTSCRAY

(Once of Verona, in Another Life)

A remarkable campaign against swearing, instituted in Verona, is claimed to have reduced bad language in that city by 75 per cent.

First Gentleman:
Corpo di Bacco, Bill I mean, dear me!
The times is surely changin'. Did yeh see
Wot's 'appened up in ole Verona now?
They're down on swearin'. Now ain't that a cow?
Remember, in our former life, 'ow we
Hit up the town with language flowin' free?

Second Gentleman:
Do I remember? 'Struth — that is to say,
Chistoforo Colomb! Them times was gay!
Reel bonzer times they was, an', strike me pink!
Verona! Wot would poor ole Shakespeare think?
The bloke 'oo made 'em swagger round the street
Servin' out lash an' language both dead neat.

First Gentleman:
Ah, Maladetta! — I mean, spare me days!
Poor ole Verona's sunk to genteel ways.
Remember when Mercutio went reel sore,
An' outed Tybalt? Blimey! 'Ow they swore!
Ole Capulet 'imself could use a curse,
An' some blokes said that Montague was worse.

Second Gentleman:
Sapristi! — I mean, Blimey! Lad, yer right;
Them was the days when we could cuss an' fight.
Even that young sonk, Romeo, could swear,
When 'e got set 'e'd fairly raise yer 'air.
Yeh rekerleck 'ow 'e let loose that day,
'E 'ad to leave 'is tart an' duck away;

First Gentleman:
Swear! Dio mio! — that is, strike a light!
'E turned the air fair purple on that night.
Sich lovely language never can I catch
In these days, even at a football match.
Wot must ole Shakespeare think, there in 'is grave —
Poor ole Verona made a wowsers' slave!

Second Gentleman:
Ah, wot a bloomin' fallin' off is there —
In ole Verona, where a bloke can't swear!

First Gentleman:
No matter, mate in that ole narrer street,
A cuss by any other name will sound as sweet.

Second Gentleman:
But these 'ere changes makes me feel reel queer.

First Gentleman:
Corpo di bloomin' Bacco! 'Ave a beer!

SLING IT!

By "THE BLOKE"

A resolution condemning slang was passed by the Anglican Synod in Melbourne yesterday.

Blimey! Ain't it gittin' tough?
Life gits 'arder day by day.
First a bloke ain't got enough
Words for wot 'e wants to say;
Then some nark, with nix to do,
Cuts vocab'laries in two.

'Ow can coots ixpress their souls?
Many a noble song is sung
By crook lips; an' music rolls
Off full many a slangy tongue.
Many a word o' wisdom's spoke
By some reel dead leery bloke.

Still in all, I gotter own,
If pure lingo we would teach,
Young kids' minds 'ad best be sown
With some dinkum slabs of speech.
Shove this motter in each book:
"Sling the slang; it's all dead crook."

ANZAC

ARMISTICE

To His Dead Cobber from The Sentimental Bloke

I'm sittin' 'ere, Mick — sittin' 'ere today,
Feelin' 'arf glum, 'arf sorter — reverent,
Thinkin' strange, crooked thorts of 'ow they say:
"The 'eads is bowed thro' all a continent";
An' wond'rin' — wond'rin' in a kind of doubt
If other coves is feelin' like I do,
Tryin' to figure wot it's all about,
An' — if it's meanin' anythin' to you.

Silence . . . The hour strikes soon thro' all the land
An' 'eads bend low. Old mate, give me your 'and.
Silence — for you, Mick, an' for blokes like you
To mark the Day — the Day you never knoo.

The Day you never knoo, nor we forget . . .
I can't tell why I'm sittin' 'ere this way,
Scrawlin' a message that you'll never get —
Or will you? I dunno. It's 'ard to say.
P'raps you'll know all about it, where you are,
An' think, "Ah, well, they ain't too bad a lot."
An' tell them other digs up on your star
That now, or nevermore, they ain't fergot.

Silence . . . Not 'ere alone, Mick — everywhere —
In city an' in country 'eads are bare.
An', in this room, it seems as if I knoo
Some friend 'oo came — Ole cobber! Is it you?

Me 'eart is full, Mick . . . 'Struth! I ain't the bloke,
As you well know, to go all soft an' wet.
Fair's fair, lad. Times I've known when you 'ave spoke
Like you was tough an' 'ard as 'ell — an' yet
Somethin' be'ind your bluff an' swagger bold
Showed all them narsty sentiments was kid.

It was that thing inside yeh, lad, wot told.
It made you go an' do the thing you did.

Silence . . . There's mothers, Mick. You never knoo
No mother. But they're prayin' for you too.
In every heart — The Boys! The Boys are there,
The Boys . . . That very name, lad, is a pray'r.

The Boys! Old cobber, I can see 'em still:
The drums are rollin' an' the sunlight gleams
On bay'nits. Men are marchin' with a will
On to the glory of their boy'ood's dreams.
Glory? You never found it that, too much.
But, lad, you stuck it — stuck it with the rest,
An' if your bearin' 'ad no soulful touch,
'Twas for *OUR* souls that you went marchin' — West.

Silence . . . The children too, Mick — little kids,
Are standin'. Not becos their teacher bids:
They've knoo no war; but they 'ave stopped their play
Becos they know, they feel it is The Day.

So may it be thro' all the comin' years.
But sorrow's gone, lad. It's not that we know.
The sobbin's passed, 'ole cobber, an' the tears,
An' well we un'erstand you'd 'ave it so.

But somethin' deeper far than that 'as come,
Somethin' a mind can't get within its bound,
Somethin' I can't explain. A man is dumb
When 'e thinks . . . Listen! 'Ear the bugles sound!

Silence!

* * * *

Well, Mick, ole cock, I dunno why I've wrote,
It's just to ease a thing inside wot says
"Sit down, you sloppy coot, an' write a note
To that ole cobber of the olden days.
'E'll know — for sure 'e'll know"." So, lad, it's done,
Work's waitin', an' a man can't get in wrong:
Our goal is still ahead. But yours is won:
That's the one thing we know, lad, an — So long.

Silence . . . It's over, Mick; so there you are.
I know you're 'appy up there on yer star.
Believe us, lad; that star shall never fall
While one is left to say, "Gawd keep 'em all!"

A MESSAGE

Armistice Day 1936

I got dreamin' that a message come in some mysterious way
From one ole pal of mine, gone West this many an' many a day,
A bloke the name of Ginger Mick, a fightin' cove I knoo.
(But 'e's Digger Corporal Mick Esquire, late A.I.F., to you)
'E got 'is on Gallipoli, an' sleeps there with the best,
Not leavin' very much be'ind, excep' one small request.
"Look after things," was all 'e said, when 'e was mortal 'urt.
Dead sure 'is mates — that's me an' you — would never do 'im dirt.

(Think of it in the Silence, with yer 'eads bowed low:
Do we keep the unspoke compact with the men we used to know?)

For I dreams it in the silence of a dark Remembrance Eve;
An' the message seems to tell me it is gettin' late to grieve.
"But if you seem to miss us still, then get the sob-stuff o'er,
An' think about the things wot we went an' fought a war.
Send up a pray'r an' drop a tear an' bend a reverent knee —
(Says Digger Corporal Ginger Mick, A.I.F., says 'e)
But is them things we fought for still the things most dear to you:
The honor an' the glory an' the mateship that we knew?"

(Think of it in the Silence, when the Last Post plays —
The splendid glimpse of Truth we 'ad, once, in the bitter days)

"Grief is a passin' compliment," the message seems to say;
But tears don't carry on the job for men that drift away.
We 'ad small time or taste for such where guns was raisin' 'ell,
When we got busy plantin' blokes an' wishin' 'em farewell.
We blowed sad music over 'em — plain Digs, or Brass 'at Knuts —
But we played a quick-step comin' back, to show we 'ad the guts.
Our speech was rough, our ways was tough — tough as our bloody game.
Are the rough, tough, lads still honored, like when the Terror came?"

(Think of it in the Silence, when their spirits hover near:
The vision and the vows that held while still the land knew fear.)

'E's sleepin' on Gallipoli. At least, 'is bones is there:
Bones worth a ton of livin' flesh that won't play fair —
Not till the Terror comes again. "An' when it does," says 'e,

If gods you've worshipped let you down, well, don't blame me."
'E's seen a lot, an' learned a lot most like, where 'e 'as gone;
An' 'eaven 'elp us when we meet if we ain't carried on.
A vulgar person, Ginger Mick, a fightin' cove I knoo —
(But Digger Corporal Ginger Mick, if you please, to you.)

(Think of it in the Silence; an', if you pray, pray deep
That all we 'ave an' all we are old loyalties shall keep.)

A SONG OF ANZAC

"WHEN I'm sittin' in me dug-out with me rifle on me knees,
An' a yowlin', 'owlin' chorus comes a-floatin' up the breeze —
Just a bit o' 'Bonnie Mary'
Or 'Long Way to Tipperary' —
Then I know I'm in Australia took an' planted overseas . . ."

SO we sang in days remembered — fateful days of pain and war —
When the young lads went forth singing, ship-bound for an unknown shore.
They were singing, ever singing, careless lads in careworn days,
Sturdy youths, but yet unblooded to red war's unholy ways.
From a land untouched by slaughter
Fared they forth across the water:
Some to Destiny's grim gateway where the scarlet poppy sways.

* * * *

"THEY were singin' on the troopship, they were singin' in the train;
When they left their land behind them they were shoutin' a refrain.
An' I'll bet they have a chorus
Gay an' glad in greetin' for us
When their bit of scrappin's over an' they sail back home again . . ."

SO we sang to dull the aching that was looming even then
When the boys went out to battle, to come back stern fighting men.
So we strove to keep hope buoyant while they lived untouched by war,
But they came back, not with singing, when those anxious days were o'er
Disillusioned and war-weary,
And, for all their smiles were cheery,
Some came bitter, some came broken, some, they came back nevermore.

AND today again they're marching, rugged veterans, grey and grave,
These, who joined the carefree chorus, shouting many an olden stave
  To the tramping cohorts' motion;
  To the rolling of the ocean;
In their singing seeking kinship that high youth must ever crave.
Aye, today again they're marching with old faith and fellowship;
Grave and grey, with memory marching, but no song lifts to the lip.
Year by year the Boys are gathered; year by year the count grows fewer;
But the flame, new-lit on Anzac, goes before them burning pure;
  And the Song of Anzac ringing
  High above them, sounding, swinging,
Tells that memory of Anzac shall endure while these endure.

* * * *

THEY are marching with the old days, with the singing in their hearts,
With the memory of mateship that for not one hour departs:
  Silent men, with sober faces,
  Marking now the vacant places
Yearly growing, yearly showing where life ends and hope re-starts.
That trimphant Song of Anzac that the living Anzac hears —
  Hears imperfectly and dimly,
  As he tramps on gravely, grimly —
Haunts the old familiar roadway he has trodden thro' the years.
Done are these with youth's vain dreaming who have yet to pay earth's price,
  These who harked to young mates singing,
  These who saw their young souls winging,
Ever singing, blithely singing, to the gates of Paradise.

BLOKES

'ERB

DO you know 'Erb? Now, there's a dinkum sport.
If football's on your mind, why, 'Erb's the sort
  To put you wise. It's his whole end an' aim.
  Keen? He's as keen as mustard on the game.
Football is in his blood. He thinks an' schemes
All through the season; talks of it an' dreams
  An' eats an' sleeps with football on his mind.
  Yes: 'Erb's a sport — the reel whole-hearted kind.

"A healthy, manly sport." That's wot 'Erb says.
You ought to see his form on football days:
  Keyed up, reel eager, eyes alight with joy,
  Full of wise schemes for his team to employ.
Knows all about it — how to kick a goal,
An' wot to do if they get in a hole.
  Enthusiasm? Why, when 'Erb gets set
  He is a sight you couldn't well forget.

There ain't a point about it he don't know —
All of the teams an' players, top to toe.
  The rules, the tricks — it's marvellous the way
  He follers — Wot? Good Lord, no, he don't play.
'Erb? Playin' football? Blimey! Have a heart!
  Aw, don't be silly. 'Erb don't have to play;
  He knows more than them players any day.

He's never had a football in his hand,
'Cept once, when it was kicked up in the stand.
  No, 'Erb ain't never played; he only sits
  An' watches 'em, an' yells, an' hoots, and splits
His sides with givin' mugs some sound advice
An' tellin' umpires thigs wot ain't too nice.
  Aw, look; your ejication ain't complete
  Till you know 'Erb. You reely ought to meet.

FRED

DO you know Fred? Now there's a man to know
  These days when politics are in the air,
An' argument is bargin' to an' fro
  Without a feller gittin' anywhere.
Fred never argues; he's too shrewd for that.
He's wise. He knows the game from A to Z.
  All politics is talkin' thro' the hat;
An' everyone is wrong — exceptin' Fred.

Fred says there ain't no sense in politics;
  Says he can't waste his time on all that rot.
Trust him. He's up to all their little tricks,
  You'd be surprised the cunnin' schemes he's got.
Fred says compuls'ry voting is a cow.
  He has to vote, or else he would be fined,
But he just spoils his paper anyhow,
  An' laughs at 'em with his superior mind.

But when a law comes in that hits Fred's purse,
  You ought to hear him then. Say, he does rouse;
Kicks up an awful row an' hurls his curse
  On every bloomin' member in the House.
He gives 'em nothin'; says they all are crook,
  All waitin' for a chance to turn their coats;
Says they are traitors; proves it by the book.
  An' can you wonder that he never votes?

Aw, say, you must know Fred. You'll hear his skite
  Upon street corners all about the place.
An' if you up an' say it serves him right,
  He answers that it ony proves his case:
Them politicians wouldn't tax him so
  Unless they were all crooked, like he said,
Where is the sense in votin' when they go
  An' rob a man like that. Hurray for Fred!

GUS

One of the bitterest complaints of Health Week is against the noisy motor cyclist, whose deliberate racketing at night is one of the banes of the modern city.

DO you know Gus? Now, he should interest you.
The girls adore him — or he thinks they do.
He owns a motor bike, not of the sort
That merely cough a little bit, or snort.
His is a fiery, detonating steed
That makes the town sit up and take some heed —
A thunderous thing, that booms and roars a treat,
With repercussions that awake the street.

That's Gus. Dead flash. One of the rorty boys,
Whose urge is to express themselves with noise,
He wakes the midnight echoes, when to sleep
We vainly strive, with detonations deep.
And Gus has visions, as he thunders by,
Of maidens who sit up in bed, and sigh,
"It's Gus! It's Gus, the he-man. What a thrill!
'Mid Jovian thunders riding up the hill!"

You can't blame Gus. He has to make a row.
He's got to get publicity somehow.
How else could he stir consciousness in us
That in this world there really is a Gus?
You can't blame Gus. But oft I long, in bed,
That some kind man would bash him on the head —
A hard, swift blow to give him pain for pain.
It would be quite safe. It couldn't hurt his brain.

BERT

DID you ever meet Bert? 'E's all over the town,
  In offices, shops an' in various places,
Cocky an' all; an' you can't keep 'im down.
  I never seen no one so lucky at races.
Backs all the winners or very near all;
  Tells you nex' day when the races are over.
'E makes quite a pot, for 'is wagers ain't small;
  An' by rights 'e 'ad ought to be livin' in clover.

But, some'ow or other — aw, well, I dunno.
  You got to admit that some fellers is funny.
'E don't dress too well an' 'is spendin' is low.
  I can't understand wot 'e does with 'is money.
'E ought to be sockin' a pretty fair share;
  An' tho' 'e will own 'e's a big money-maker,
'E don't seem to save an' 'e don't seem to care
  If 'e owes a big wad to 'is butcher an' baker.

'E don't tell you much if you meet on the course;
  But after it's over 'e comes to you grinnin',
Shows you 'is card where 'e's marked the first 'orse,
  An' spins you a wonderful tale of 'is winnin'.
Can't make 'im out, 'e's so lucky an' that.
  Knows ev'ry owner an' trainer an' jockey;
But all of 'is wagerin's done on 'is pat.
  Won't spill a thing, even tho' 'e's so cocky.

Oyster, that's Bert. 'E's as close as a book.
  But sometimes I've come on 'im sudden an' saw 'im
Lip 'angin' down an' a reel 'aggard look,
  Like all the woes in the world come to gnaw 'im.
But, soon as 'e sees you, 'e brightens right up.
"Picked it again, lad!" 'e sez to you, grinnin'.
"A fiver at sevens I 'ad in the Cup!
  That's very near sixty odd quid that I'm winnin'."

Mystery man — that's 'is style for a cert,
  Picks the 'ole card, yet 'e's shabby and seedy;
'E must 'ave some sorrer in secrit, ole Bert —
  Some drain on 'is purse wot is keepin' 'im needy.
A terrible pity. Some woman, no doubt.
  No wonder 'e worries in secrit an' souses.
If I 'ad 'is winnin's, year in an' year out,
  Why I'd own a Rolls Royce an' a terris of 'ouses.

IN THE GARDEN

BEGGARS OF THE BUSH

What I Saw In My Garden

WE have always made it a matter of justice that we should feed the magpies as well as the other and lowlier birds about this little clearing in the forest.

We are meticulous about this, because we know that appearances are often deceptive, and, although magpies generally, with their aggressive aspect and fearless habit, seem well able to look after and fend for themselves, one never knows what injustice may be done by making distinctions in one's charity to the birds.

So we fed the magpies regularly, but they received little of our sympathy until there came upon the scene one cold, autumn day, John Silver and his mate, Limpy.

I don't know whether fellow feeling had drawn these two strange birds together, or whether they had been mates before disaster overtook them; but the curious fact remained that they were each possessed of only one leg!

In each case, it was to be surmised, a barbarous rabbit-trap had accounted for the other limb. John Silver's had been severed high up so that nothing remained but a pathetic stump. His wife, Limpy, had lost little more than a foot.

* * * *

OF course, the sentimentalist of the household was roused to loud wailings when she first beheld this pair of avian cripples, and I will admit that they certainly did look forlorn — or else were putting up a rather good bluff. It was hard to say which.

John Silver's method of approaching sustenance was especially provoking of pity. On his one good leg he would hop rather painfully to within striking distance of some proffered morsel of food; then he would sit down on his stomach and, by some strange means that I have never been able to discover, wriggle forward to the food.

Limpy was more spry on her remaining limb; nor did her brown eye hold that piteous glance of appeal that came into John Silver's whenever he chanced to catch the eye of the almoner.

Well, of course, special arrangements had to be made for these two pensioners. They had, for instance, to have a separate feeding time when other, and younger and stronger magpies were not there to bully them.

* * * *

YET, in spite of all precautions, brawls and piratical raids were frequent, and frequently, too, a wild and angry squawking in the back paddock brought us hurriedly out of doors to the rescue of our pair of invalids. Or rather, that is what we thought at the time.

"We shall never be able to save them!" said the sentimentalist. "Those hefty young ones will kill them eventually. The law of the wild is atrociously cruel."

I was of much the same opinion and had foreseen for Silver and Limpy a very brief remainder to their mortal span, until —

Well, yesterday morning, I happened to be strolling through the rather dense scrub that adjoins this clearing when I heard a wild hullabaloo that told of magpies in dire distress — almost in mortal agony.

"This is the end," thought I, "of Silver and Limpy." And I crept slowly through the scrub to see what I could see.

What I did see was this: John Silver, full of rage and fury, on top of a hefty young bird who was yelling for mercy, while, a few yards away, Limpy was dealing with another aggressor even more strenuously! Severed feet or missing legs seemed to incommode them not in the least.

These indiscreet interlopers had raided Silver's private and particular feeding grounds. They had to be dealt with. They were being dealt with.

* * * *

I HAVE not yet said anything at home concerning what I witnessed yesterday. And I doubt if I ever shall.

For that look which John Silver gives me out of his brown eye every time we meet has lost all of its pathetic appeal.

It says now unmistakably, eloquently: "Now, see here, between friends — between mates, don't say anything about what you saw. It would absolutely cruel my pitch. And you know what a good wicket I'm on."

Well, who'd do that to a magpie — even to an arrant hypocrite of a magpie? Not I. Or is it "Not me"?

REVERIE IN A GARDEN

I'D never known these peaceful hours
Till on a summer long ago
I won the gift of friendly flowers,
And learned their ways, and came to know
From what drab earth may beauty grow.

But since I learned, as might the bees
A garden's myriad mysteries
Of alchemy when seeds are sown,
I've known delights I'd never known.

Endless delights the garden holds:
A still pool fringed by marigolds;
A rose-lined walk; a shaded lawn;
A dew-wet iris in the dawn —

The gift of color tulips win
In the dark night; how seeds begin
In downy cradles, snugly set;
The incense of one violet.

"A garden is a lovesome thing,"
The poet sang. Well might he sing.
Knowing what love and loveliness
One simple garden may express.

"God walks in mine," the poet cried.
By whom shall such words be denied?
Never by him whose secret heart
Holds all a garden may impart.

Had I the choice to walk with kings
Or walk alone where lilac swings
Its censers, wreathed in wondrous scent,
I'd walk alone, and know content.

Yet, might I walk alone? He knows
Who, where some well-loved garden grows,
Feels, at a flash, his heart set free
In beauty-bidden ecstasy —

As if, unheralded, unguessed,
An accolade of peace had crowned —
A sudden gift of grace had blest
The garden's glory, and he found
His feet on consecrated ground.

DAHLIAS

WHILE Autumn spills her loveliness
Where living jewels grow,
Full gratitude would I express
That, many years ago,
From Swedish shores the good Herr Dahl set out for Mexico.

IN Mexico, old Mexico,
In days gone in the gloom
Of centuries, lost years ago,
A man long in his tomb —
An Aztec garden-lover — toiled to make a garden bloom.

AND so — in fancy I prefer
To dream — by bed and bower
This ancient Aztec amateur
Spent many a toilful hour,
Until, one day, there bloomed for him a truly magic flower.

TOO soon the ruthless Spaniard came,
Man's progress to impress,
Till that old race was but a name.
Yet, out of death's distress,
Seed wafted from the magic bloom into the wilderness.

AND hither, after many a year
Had shaped the land anew,
Came Dahl, to rediscover here
The bloom an Aztec grew,
And rescue from the wilderness beauty for me and you.

NOW, when I walk the garden's ways
In this, a newer land,
And see the wondrous colors blaze
And burn at every hand.
I bless good Dahl and that vague ghost who all this magic planned.

BY bordered path and garden bed
Glow blossoms great and small,
Huge blooms lift each a lovely head
On stems serenely tall
O'er clustered pompones crimped and shaped each to a perfect ball.

AND now, when Autumn comes to boast
Of joys that Summer missed,
I would stand forth and pledge a toast
To Dahl, the botanist,
And that strange being lost in time, the Aztec alchemist.

WARMBATS

The Gardener's Foe

WARMBATS," said my friend, the bushman, "is gettin' to be fair dawgs."

Although dark pigs would seem to me to provide a more fitting comparison, I hastened to agree.

"Warmbats," continued the bushman, "got no gumption. Net out rabbits an' they stays out. They got savvy enough to know they ain't wanted; but warmbats is too thick-headed to take a hint."

Again I agreed; for I had been having recent experience of the stolid wombat's ways.

With the idea of experimenting in a little landscape gardening I decided the other day to enclose an acre or two of land that for many years has been disputed territory so far as the wombats and myself are concerned. I had made half-hearted attempts previously to indicate that wombats were not welcome in this paddock; but, as the bushman says, they are slow to take hints. They sneered at my prohibitions and walked through my puny defences with the inexorable urge and passionless persistence of military tanks.

With the garden in view, wire-netting seemed to be indicated; so we ran up a strong fence, burying six inches of the netting in the earth and stapling it securely to every post. At three separate points the fence intersected three well defined wombat tracks, used regularly by these persistent prowlers upon their nightly sallies.

* * * *

ON the evening that we finished the fence, I removed the temporary guards from trees and flower plots, confident that my fort was impregnable.

Next morning, at two points, my nice, new netting had been ruthlessly uprooted. Evidence showed that one simple motion of a powerful forepaw had breached the defences, and the wombats walked through to chew my eschscholtzias and sup prodigiously on foxglove and perennial phlox. Their troubles about digitalis — it serves them merely as a gentle stimulant.

Called into conference, the bushman suggested sunken logs.

"Warmbats," he opined, "are bull-headed cows. You got to wear 'em down."

A trench was dug along the fence's length and logs from twelve to eighteen feet in length, needing the combined strength of two hefty men to move them, were laid along the fence's foot and the earth well-rammed on top.

Next morning two neat tunnels ran beneath the logs on the line of two of the wombat tracks. At the third point a huge log, heavy enough to tax the thews of a strong man, had been bodily unearthed and contemptuously tossed aside.

Appealed to once more, the bushman began to look grave.

"Warmbats," he decided, not without a hint of admiration, "are pretty tough birds all right, all right."

* * * *

HE then suggested a more deeply sunken barricade at the various points of entry. As he explained, wombats, in one aspect, resemble a certain type of politician; they are dogged possessors of single-track minds. Yet unlike politicians, they know nothing of compromise. The motto of the wombat nation seems to be, "Wombats turn aside for nought." If they can not pass over an obstacle they will barge through it or burrow under; but to deviate from the beaten path is to be dishonored in wombatian eyes.

They have been known to spend nights tunnelling beneath a recently fallen tree that crossed their track when, by turning aside for six or eight feet they could have walked unhindered around the severed butt.

With much labor, we put down the sunken palisades but, alas, one at least of the raiders seemed to be the possessor of a devious and original turn of mind unworthy of a true wombat. Finding his way barred, he simply went along the fence and put in another subway.

Importuned once more, the bushman had nothing further to suggest save special traps or a night's vigil with a rifle. Mere shot, he explained, would "bounce orf the cow's 'ide like 'ail-stones."

I slyly suggested that, should we bag one this way, some larder might be replenished wiht succulent meat.

The bushman snorted as I expected he would.

"May as well ask a man," he said, "to eat snake, with bardee grubs for a dressin'."

It is one of those queer bush prejudices, difficult to understand.

A man who has rabbit too often on the menu is regarded with pitying suspicion; but one who habitually dines on wombat courts social degradation in a forest community. Yet I have been told by those who took the social and gastric risk that the flesh of a young wombat is very like prime young pork. The mere sight of a scaly veteran, however, would repel a cannibal.

I hesitate to take the last advice of my bush friend. Even a wombat has some right to life and the pursuit of stolid happiness.

I have, at intervals, tried with no success (1) pointed stakes, (2) broken glass, (3) a notice warning trespassers.

Wombats don't care.

I have toyed with the idea of sinking a moat around my domain with drawbridge and portcullis complete; but the objective seems hardly worth it.

Meantime those "bull-headed cows" that are "pretty tough birds" and are "gettin' to be fair dawgs" continue nightly to chew the sorry remnants of my eschscholtzias.

I think I shall abandon the idea of a landscape garden and persevere with the nucleus of a private zoo instead.

BIRDLAND ON THE DOLE

Hard Days For Robins

THE weather-wise up here in the mountain country amongst the big gums are talking of records. Even the oldest inhabitant admits that "he has never seen the likes before."

"Thirty-three frosts," he says, "since May the first, an' fourteen of 'em without a break. If that aint a record, I'll go 'he'."

In my own experience of over twenty years here, I have never before known more than five consecutive nights of frost. Three frosts and then a rain is the general average in a normal winter in this part of the forest.

But the present frosty sequence has begun to upset the balance of nature. Flowering trees are beginning to put forth tentative blossom. Surprised young leaves peep forth inquiringly from deciduous plants; and the birds, deceived by the glorious sunny days into incipient and reluctant spring song, are beginning to think seriously of housekeeping.

They seem almost convinced that a winter has unaccountably gone missing somewhere.

* * * *

THE sunlit days are ideally beautiful — tragically beautiful when one remembers the conditions in drier areas of the State.

But it is the birds who seem to be having the worst time of it here. For them glorious days fail to compensate for the grub shortage. I don't know what has happened to the grubs and worms and other dainties of the avian menu, but they have become suddenly scarce: either perishing in frosty nights or digging deeper in earth in search of warmth.

The birds are equally nonplussed and are rapidly becoming mendicants — diffident at first but, with the discovery that free food is to be had for the asking, gradually assertive and at times positively imperative.

A RATHER confident grey thrush began the daily procession to the door. He (or she) was the first to be offered a morsel in the way of charity one morning when he had given up foraging and sat disconsolate by the door.

He came again and was fed. Within a very few days he began to look upon the daily dole as his unquestionable right.

At precisely nine o'clock every morning after frost he comes to the branches of a Japanese plum tree and whistles once — a loud, musical note that permits of only one interpretation: "Here I am. Where's my breakfast?"

Should the almoner be late, the calls become louder and more frequent, and further delay leads to an outcry that cannot be ignored.

A handful of varied scraps is scattered on the lawn and he dives immediately and breakfasts unafraid, fully aware that he enjoys the privilege and protection of a favorite.

His departure, replete and musically grateful, is the signal for the general descent. First the currawongs, whose shrewd, white eyes have been watching from adjacent gums, secure their provender on the cash-and-carry system, since they know that, because of their greed, they may not linger.

After them come the more diffident satin birds who also carry away and eat their food in private, but as a matter of preference and good manners.

* * * *

THE magpies, those proud and arrogant birds, refuse to eat with the rabble, and insist upon a separate meal time at another hour of the day.

But, with the disappearance of the larger birds, the small fry come clamoring for their share, for all have been watching and waiting in the bushes round about.

First of these the impertinent yellow robins who have long since learned that to perch cheekily upon a forefinger insures one a full and uninterrupted meal while others catch as catch can in the general scramble. Blue wrens hop about the banquet's edge; scrub wrens, chats and tits watch their chance to snatch a morsel, and so, until the last small songster has been satisfied.

Then all go about their own lawful occasions, and no bird begs about the door for the rest of that day.

For there is this to be said of the birds: As soon as the frozen earth is in fit state for foraging they prefer to stick to the job, however ill repaid in grubs and other delicacies. After only one frostless night they prefer work to free sustenance, excepting only that aggressively mendicant grey thrush, who seems to have entirely lost his self respect and become determined to loaf on the government for the rest of his feathered life.

GREY THRUSH AT THE DOOR

"SWE-E-ET! Swe-e-et!" Low at first and flattering,
Full of soft seductiveness on a wheedling note.
Who comes in mercy now, crumbs of comfort scattering
For a grey bird pleading from a cold, cold throat?
Just a shred of tallow-fat, just a scrap of meat!
Grey Thrush is at the door. "Swe-e-et! Swe-e-et!"

GREY bird, friendly bird, merry bird in summer time,
For summer is a merry time, full of tuneful mirth.
Sunny days are singing days. But winter is a glummer time
With lean days of scant fare; frost has locked the earth.
Song goes as sun goes, and harshly drives the sleet.
Where comes the almoner? "Swe-e-et! Swe-e-et!"

"SWEET! Sweet!" Now it grows imperious:
A short call, a loud call, impatience in its tone.
Why am I left lingering? See, my plight is serious.
A poor bird all forlorn, starving and alone.
Grey Thrush is a-hungering, begging scraps to eat.
It's far beyond my breakfast time! "Sweet! Sweet!!"

NOW a footstep on the floor. Now a sudden fluttering.
And Grey Thrush is waiting there beside the open door.
Kookaburra cocks an eye; greedily he's muttering;
But grey bird is first to swoop upon the proffered store,
A scrap of song in gratitude, then up, and off, away.
And the mendicant has vanished till another frosty day.

THE AMENDE HONORABLE

The Story of a Conscience

I HAVE never regarded the possession of a tender conscience as in any sense an asset. Even for the pure in heart, because of the need for perpetual watchfulness lest it be inadvertently offended, the thing becomes a liability. While for the venal, the indulger of slothful subterfuge and the follower of paths that lead along the line of least resistance a tender conscience can and does become a thorn in the flesh, a viper in the bosom and a positive pain in the neck.

I fervently wish that mine were tougher.

For that super-sensitive thing that I recognise as a conscience, inhabiting some dank cell in the dark hinterland of my being has been nagging at me — positively nagging at me day and night for a week because I have been unjust to a dog. Can you believe it?

If you own a tender conscience you can; if you cannot, it merely reveals you as one of those extremely tough eggs with a conscience made of synthetic rubber reinforced with spring steel, and you will probably get on in life.

* * * *

ANYHOW, I am going to own up here and now and try to get a little peace. For I am sick (for one thing) of being discovered around remote corners being abjectly apologetic to a four-footed friend whose persistent attitude toward me is one of disillusionment and dumb disdain.

Some time ago I told of a dog who had watched a heap of blue-gum firewood for over a year because in the beginning he had seen a small black rabbit seek sanctuary there. I told how, when the stack came at last to be removed, the dog became suddenly interested, carefully following each barrowful, watching the withdrawal of every stick with meticulous attention, only to find in the end (so I said) when the last of the wood was shifted, that no rabbit was there.

I told also of the dog's comical disgust, of his loss of further interest, and I aggravated the offence by referring to his canine reasoning as "absurd". And when we told visitors of the amusing episode they laughed immoderately at the idiotic dog and his fatuous faith in the permanence of rabbits. "Fancy! After a whole year! It was too ridiculous."

Meantime, as they laughed (and I, perjured hypocrite, laughed with them) inwardly I squirmed and writhed secretly under the prickings and proddings, the intolerable nudges and naggings of that most unprofitable and wholly damnable incubus, my tender conscience.

* * * *

AND now it drives me to reluctant confession; for, as a matter of fact —

But let me begin at the beginning and recount the whole truth as briefly as may be.

More than a year ago the dog, Tam, and I had a short and merry chase after a small black rabbit that had somehow got inside the protective netting that encloses the residential block, only to drive him to cover in a crevice at the very bottom of the blue-gum stack.

Since nothing could dislodge bunny, save the removal of virtually the whole stack, the household was much concerned, and the housewife saw the whole of her cherished garden vulnerable to the assaults of a vowed and voracious vegetarian.

But I was not going to shift that wood, it was not yet dry enough for use, and the gardener had other things to do. So, after investigation, I announced finally that the black rabbit had left the stack and returned as he had come to his native habitat. I staked my reputation on it.

But still the housewife doubted. Choice carnations were being ruthlessly chewed, gladioli gobbled, if not by the black rabbit, then by what?

So the thing developed into a year-long argument. Tender annuals were disappearing; but, basing my man-made logic on reasonable grounds, I pointed out that no rabbit could inhabit a small hole in a wood stack month after month and reveal not hide nor hair of him. Preposterous! Housewife, dog and raided garden notwithstanding, the contention was absurd!

* * * *

AND now for the shameface truth.

While the last of that blue-gum was being shifted I viewed the proceedings from an upstairs casement. When the gardener (and Tam) had come down to the house with the penultimate barrow load, and but a few sticks remained, I saw, emerging from beneath those few sticks an extremely fat black rabbit — fat with the vitamins of heaven knows what choice carnations; sleek with the succulent juices of nemesia, godetia, eschscholtzia, and a hundred precious plants.

He slipped swiftly from the dwindling stack and hid in a

rhododendron clump near a wide gate.

My reputation was at stake! At all costs my face must be saved!

Hastily I sneaked downstairs, set the gate wide open, and gently shoo-ed the black rabbit through into his customary bush. Then gently latching the gate, I wished him good hunting and sneaked back upstairs before the gardener and the dog could return.

So now the truth is out. There was a rabbit after all, and Tam, the dog, was right, his vigil justified.

I withdraw and apologise.

No more, when visitors laugh immoderately at Tam's supposed stupidity (and there is nothing a dog resents so much as being laughed at), no more when he sneaks abjectly around a corner of the house, ears and tail a-droop, shall I have to follow him with pleas and excuses, only to meet two brown eyes brimming with tears of dumb reproach.

I shall read this to him when it is printed; and, because he is a dog, he will forgive.

RHODODENDRONS

Rhododendrons are now beginning to bloom gloriously in various mountain regions of Victoria. Of these beautiful flowers, the late Blamire Young, that poet in water-color, once said that "they hold the quality of tears".

NONE save a poet's eye marked this, concealed;
None save a poet's mind conceived the phrase
Whereat, all suddenly, is there revealed
A hidden beauty to our wondering gaze,
Until, reluctantly, grows the belief
That ecstasy can be so near to grief.

The quality of tears, beauty so rare;
Perfection drawn to such a splendid height
Of loveliness, that pain is almost there;
And, as the miracle glows in our sight,
Deep in our hearts we know when all is done
In the last end are joy and sorrow one.

Now in this garden are great torches lit
Of many colors, flaming to the sky.
Song is abroad where honeyeaters flit
'Mid cherry-blossom, and the plaintive cry
Of cuckoos weaves and wafts, till one is caught
In breathless wonder at the beauty wrought.

Gaze deep into the heart of this one bloom,
Into the dewy tenderness set there,
Gaze long until the heart finds no more room
For foolish doubt, or hating, or despair.
Gaze on this miracle sprung from dull sod,
And know their folly who live doubting God.

The quality of tears. Yet not the tears
Of human bitterness that finds no worth
In life; of weariness or human fears
That glimpse no hope in all this harried earth,
But tears won out of ecstasy too sweet
For those who walk the earth with leaden feet.

Wisdom lies here; a wisdom far beyond
The lore of sages striving toilfully
For those hard truths that bring nought save despond
To luckless mortals lacking eyes to see
Wisdom the poet found these many years —
Found in a flower's rare quality of tears.

SPRING POEM - OPUS 175,631

POET'S CORNER
11th August, 1937.

DEAR SIR,
Your esteemed communication of 27th ult. is
To hand, and contents duly noted.
We wish to advise, however, that your tendency to exult is
A little premature and not entirely promoted
By the established facts of the case
At above-mentioned time and place.
Your valued order, however, per your Mr Smith,
Is duly despatched herewith.

IN re. one (1 only) Spring,
Advent of: We now proceed, as requested, to sing,
At current market rates, and in a somewhat minor key —
Also c.i.f., in odd lots. E. & O.E. —
A little pastoral thing
As under:
Wintertime activity
With the usual seasonal proclivity
Toward frost, hail, rain, snow and/or thunder,
Now shows a markedly downward tendency;
While Jonquils (sales 6d to 6½d.) are in the ascendancy
A new high for Bath Songs is in sight,
And the outlook for Flappers (ordinary and preferred) is increasingly bright.

SAP (ex Autumn dividend) is rising;
But Skies are dull, according to latest advising.
Birds (various) exhibit increased activity a-wing;
There is a growing demand,
As per latest reports to hand,
For Fluff, Feathers, odd lots of Straw, Bark and Second-hand String;
And all building materials and those for nest-lining
Show no signs of declining.
Buds, Bath Robes, Bird-songs, Butterflies, Bees and Batsmen have a tendency to firm;
But there is a marked despondency in the movements of the Early Worm.

IN gold stocks
Wattles display a decided inclination to pull up their socks.
Rhododendrons at present are quiet,
Tho' likely later to cause a riot.
Nevertheless,
We desire, sir, to express
The need for caution in early trading.
According to our latest bill of lading
Early shipments of Balmy Morns, Golden Eves, Soft Zephyrs and
Young Man's Fancies are likely to be poor,
And the position is by no means secure.
According to confidential advices to hand a
Movement to boost all such
Is very much
The result of poetic propaganda;
And any attempt to bull the market in Divine Afflatus (No
Liability)
Would, in our opinion, be utter futility.
Thanking you for your esteemed patronage once again,
I, sir, have the honour to remain
Ever at your service with mind and pen
As poetic and seasonal guide.
(Families supplied)
Yours very sincerely,
DEN.
(Manager, Vernal Dept.)

OLD TOWN TYPES

THE OLD TOWN

FIERCE on the wheat-sown Mallee plain
   The ruthless summer suns burned down,
And dust-storms, heralding the rain,
Swept thro' the street and on again,
   While tradesfolk cursed in the old white town.
Of sand and lime-stone stoutly built,
She'd lived to prosper and to wilt,
   Because, as all wiseacres knew,
   "They went and brought that railway thro'."

Deep-voiced, bewhiskered townsfolk these,
   Remnant of pioneering days,
Full of high tales and memories
Of wild, rough work and wilder sprees,
   When coach and teamster went their ways;
When men pushed out to newer land
And cash came easy to the hand —
   And went: The golden days men knew
   "Before they put that railway thro'."

Yet even in those days of stress —
   Or seeming stress — the old town knew
Nothing of want or wretchedness;
For wealth was there and work to bless
   All men who sought them work to do.
To me, a child in those far years,
Now as a time-dimmed dream appears
   The olden life that once I knew
   After the railway wandered thro'.

Like myths in some long-fabled tale —
   Figures and scenes to conjure with
They seem. Yet, 'spite the deepening veil,

Their memories grow never stale:
  Big George, the lumper; Toll, the smith;
Long John, the snob — long have they slept
While suns burned down and dust-storm swept
  Across the Mallee plains they knew
  Before men brought the railway thro'.

RED MATT

HE gleaned all the gossip and he gathered all the news,
  Mad Matt, the carrier, delivering the grub;
He knew the trooper's tattle and he knew the parson's views,
  The gossip at the station-yard, the gossip at the pub.
That high-pitched voice of his, the loudest voice in town,
  That shrewd blue eye of his, with humor all a-gleam —
Old Red Matt, with his cabbage-tree hat,
  His trolley, and his two-horse team.

Driving down the main street a-clatter with his load,
  The great red beard of him blowing out behind:
"Hear about that accident's mornin' up the road
  Hear about the gold rush at Joe Scott's find?
Warmish sort o' day we got; thirsty weather this.
  Got a bag o' spuds for you — Dang! Fergot the cream!"
Says old Red Matt with his cabbage-tree hat,
  And his trolley, and his two-horse team.

Mad Matt, the carrier, standing at the bar:
  "Well here's a go, boys. Got to get along.
Seven pints I've had today and still to travel far.
  Drink fast and drive fast, yeh can't go wrong.
Fill 'em up again, boss, and shove it on the slate.
  Half-a-ton aboard today — just tipped the beam,"
Says old Red Matt with the cabbage-tree hat,
  And his trolley, and his two-horse team.

Sudden were his wild ways, sudden, too, his end.
  Jumped to grab a bolting team with kiddies in the trap;
And they picked up Mad Matt, everybody's friend,
  Silent now and broken; and they said, "Brave chap.
Wild an' all," they said of him, "always was a white man."
  And they laid him, with a blessing, where his old mates dream,
Saying, "So long, Matt, with your cabbage-tree hat,
  And your trolley, and your two-horse team."

LAH-DI-DA LANE

IN the old town traditions — as greybeards will explain —
One epic tale immortalises Lah-di-dah Lane,
Clerk to a local wheat-buyer in the railway yard.
Some deemed him just a "masher", but a few said "knowing card" —
With his waxed moustache, his monocle, his grey "hard-hitter" hat,
His braided coat of black "Berlin," his lavender cravat,
His buttoned boots and finger-ring and thin Malacca cane —
Oh, a sight on pleasant Sundays was our Lah-di-dah Lane.

His manners were meticulous, his smile so softly sweet
That he soon became the butt of every urchin in our street.
But he took their banter calmly, and his brow wore ne'er a frown
Til the bully, Turk Trevanion, caused a scandal in the town.
A loud-mouthed blusterer was Turk, a crude, sardonic lout
Who made a set at Lah-di-dah, but failed to draw him out
Till he used, in ladies' hearing, words both blasphemous and vain:
Then, "I'll meet you on the wiver flat," said Lah-di-dah Lane.

Discreetly on that Sabbath day the word was passed about,
Till half the town came to the flat to see poor Lane pass out;
And a few expressed their pity; but the most of them were there
To watch in masculine contempt as, with most tender care
He laid aside his monocle, his grey "hard-hitter" hat,
His braided coat, his collar and his lavender cravat;
And on the pile he neatly laid his thin Malacca cane.
"Now then, I'll thettle you, you thwine!" lisped Lah-di-dah Lane.

Of that Homeric battle townsmen talk with bated breath;
For Lah-di-dah in action proved a streak of sudden death.
His straight lefts and upper-cuts revealed amazing form,
Till Turk, a battered, bleeding wreck, went down before the storm.
Then Lane resumed his monocle, his grey, "hard-hitter" hat,
His collar and his braided coat, his lavender cravat,
And under Turk's incarmined nose wagged his Malacca cane:
"Take that, you bwutal bwawler!" murmured Lah-di-dah Lane.

SERGEANT MAT McGILLICUDDY

KING of all the town, gaoler, censor, too,
Bane of heavy sinners doing things they shouldn't do,
Terror of the cattle-duffers in the northern scrubs,
Keeping watch on criminals, cautioning the pubs
On those brief hours, in old days, when laws forbade their beer,
Looming forth on court-days, a Nemesis severe —
Oh, a martinet and master in the art of keeping peace
Was Matthew Mark McGillicuddy, Sergeant of Police.

How the gleaming metal jingled, how the polished leather shone
When Sergeant Mat. McGillicuddy put his war-paint on:
Skin-tight corded riding breeches, spur and shoulder-strap,
Cartridge case, revolver, and a smart, peaked cap,
A black "imperial" that wagged beneath his stiff moustache —
Authority personified — he cut a heavy dash
With his boots and buttons shining and his coat without a crease —
Matthew Mark McGillicuddy, Sergeant of Police.

On race-days and show-days, when strangers sought the town,
The Sergeant was a stern man, and terrible his frown.
But he had scant use on off-days for his little gaol of tin,
Save when, to keep the town's repute, he ran some roysterer in;
To come the "morning after" with a foaming pot of beer:
"'Tis agin the regulations; but I want no corpses here.
You perishing with heat an' thirst to but a spot of grease.
An' me firewood there needs splittin'," said the Sergeant of Police.

Then they made him an inspector in the city one sad day;
But he had a glorious "send off" before he went away —
One night of wild carousal that gave scandal for a week,
But the man sent to replace him was a truckler and a sneak,
A plague to petty sinners, a peeping Tom in pubs;
But a jest among the cattle-duffers in the northern scrubs.
So we missed the human touch that lurked beneath the blustering frown
Of Matthew Mark McGillicuddy — king of our old town.

MRS FELIX DONNETT

MRS FELIX DONNETT was a lady of renown.
For ten years her husband was the mayor of the town;
For ten years she queened it as our local social light;
And "everything she did, my dear", was very, VERY right.
But the mayoral pomp sat lightly on old Felix, sly but sprightly,
And about his civic earnestness shrewd townspeople had their "doots";
But not of Mrs Donnett, with the bugles on her bonnet,
And her dolman, and her bustle, and elastic-sided boots.

Oh, a very proper lady with a very proper mind
Was she, like Queen Victoria, and exceedingly refined.
For the good Queen was her model, tho' her ideals were confused;
Still, she and Queen Victoria were not easily amused,
For she lacked all sense of humor; but she had a nose for rumor —
Spicy rumor; and a dragon 'mid the other female "plutes"
Loomed Mrs Felix Donnett, with bugles on her bonnet,
Her dignity, her dolman, and her Aunt Jemima boots.

And woe betide the romping maid whose ways she counted lax.
One roguish glance, one titter, brought "the dragon" on her tracks.
Her? Fast, mai deah? A minx, mai deah! If you but knew it all!
And Ai pity her poor mothah; but, of cawse, Ai could not call."
Then the dingle-dangles trembled 'mid the matrons there assembled
As heads were tossed, and lips compressed. "And men, of cawse, are brutes!"
Hissed Mrs Felix Donnett, with the bugles on her bonnet,
And her beadings, and her bustle, and her Aunt Jemima boots.

When I am moved to tolerance in this "unmoral age"
I take the family album out and turn each yellowed page;
And straightway I am chastened, and my moral tone comes back,
As I browse 'mid whiskered dandies and meek matrons garbed in black,
With their fal-de-rals and flounces. Then, from out the page there pounces
Mother Grundy; and my turpitude is blasted at the roots
By the glare of Mrs Donnett and the bugles on her bonnet,
And her dolman, and her bustle, and her Aunt Jemima boots.

MR BLADES THE BUTCHER

MR BLADES, the butcher, was a large and beefy man,
"Best him at a cattle deal," 'twas said, "no other can."
He ate a lot and drank a lot and had a lot to say,
And he jollied all the ladies in his large and airy way.
His family was numerous, and helped him in "the trade,"
And townsfolk had a deal to say of money that they made.
But Mr Blades just went his way, and had his bit of fun;
And joked about his appetite, his girth, or else his "run."

His "run" — a stretch of scrubland at the back of Connor's place —
Was a joke about the district; for it did not bear a trace
Of building or improvement. Yet some said Mr Blades
Had ambitions as a squatter, and a secret scorn for "trades" . . .
Then the cattle duffers started in the district. Connors raved,
But folk said it was wonderful how Mr Blades behaved.
Tho' he lost a hundred stores one night. But soon began the rows
When people in the town began to lose domestic cows.

Police surprised the gang one night out in the mulga shades,
And took the lot, red-handed, with their leader — Mr Blades.
Of course, the trial stirred our town, as nothing's stirred it since;
But when bad Blades got "three years hard," he did not even wince.
His family still strove to carry on the butcher's shop,
And sent out bills as usual. But soon they had to stop,
For folk refused to pay them, and demanded with some heat:
"Think you can charge for selling us our milkers back as meat?"

When Mr Blades came out of gaol, he did not seem ashamed;
A little thinner now, perhaps, but not the least bit tamed.
He told the folk he'd paid his debts, and so, by gum, should they.
So he summoned all his debtors, and his debtors had to pay.
"For our own thieved and slaughtered cows!" wailed these bewildered folk.
But Mr Blades, the butcher, had his last and richest joke,
And, on the day he left the town, people who saw him said
He looked the picture of content — so beefy, large, and red.

MR BODGE THE BANKER

MR BODGE, the banker, was a power in the land;
His city bank had granted him an autocratic hand;
For our town was most remote from commerce centres then,
And only Mr Bodge could know who were our solid men.
So Mr Bodge within his bank reigned with a pride immense,
And rich men and poor men, they paid him deference;
For who could know when droughts would come to jeopardise some plan?
And one word from Mr Bodge might save or sink a man.

He shone among the "silvertails," a leading social light,
Well dressed, well groomed and painfully polite.
He entertained the Governor, when he was in our town,
Magistrates and M.P.'s and others of renown.
In full beards and top hats, with such a fancy spread
That the fat cook at Flynn's pub went nearly off her head —
Cold collations, caviare, foods till then unknown.
And all were sure that Mr Bodge had money of his own.

He beamed on Peter Connor when he came into the bank,
For Connor was our squatter and a man of social rank.
He beamed on all the "silvertails" of his exclusive set;
But he frowned on cocky farmers who were over-long in debt.
"My bank considers character," he'd sternly say to those.
"If you can't pay the fifty pounds, I fear we must foreclose."
And, tho' small men called him a snob, most of the town agreed
That Mr Bodge, tho' hard at times, was very just indeed.

He once went on extended leave, and all the town's elect
Gave him a champagne send-off. 'Twas the least one might expect.
But when he overstayed his leave there was a mighty din,
The bank sent it inspectors up and called its money in —
Or tried to. But old Connor failed, and Collins at the store,
The chemist and the auctioneer and half a dozen more.
And men long talked with bated breath of that depression dire
When Mr Bodge, the banker, left the old town in the mire.

BOBBY J. AND MR SHAKESPEARE

I THINK I mentioned before that, if democracy prevails till he is a man, my young friend, Bobby J., is destined to have a brilliant commercial career. Indeed, he is assured of material success under any social system or form of government; for he is of a type which, fortunate or unfortunate, makes its own opportunities and has its eye fixed eternally on the "main chance".

Quite early in life he will be marked out by that peculiar mass prophecy which automatically selects the "coming man" who is "bound to succeed".

His acquisition of a bicycle, earned with a series of unique centenary articles on the history of our State, will perhaps be remembered. In his later correspondence I have sensed a vague nosing about for further opportunities for profit.

In his latest letter the jubilant note, ingenuously camouflaged under an assumption of gloom, told me that he had at last hit upon a plan to make duty the slave of his desire and snatch profit from the reluctant hands of destiny.

* * * *

"DEAR UNCLE (he writes), — Thank you very much for the bicicle tube. It was a great surprise for me to get it specially when I told you how my mother said you were not to be asked to send it so I never did.

"But now I got it of course it would be very rude of me to send it back because we are taught always to be polite to everybody even to our relations so thats what I am and even if it is not such a good tube as the other brand I should be very thankful for it which I am.

"So now I can ride my bicicle about all over the shop instead of listening to my old wireless

which is prak — practikly bust — burst account of how it is an old battery set nearly wore out with no volume at all.

"And when I spoke to my father about how it won't come out real loud he said that was his ideel of a wireless so long as it gave him the crect time.

"And when I spoke to my father about some very cheap parts what I could build a real loud electric set he said at first it might be a good idear to get them and keep me quiet for a few days.

* * * *

"SO there's a nice sort of a father for you. And then him telling me to save up for it out of my own pocket money which is just a measly sixpence a week for messiges and lorns and things.

"I think sometimes that very likely my father is a pretty unsyn — insimpythetic parient.

"And now dear uncle what do you think. Amongst all my other troubles they have gone and put more work on us at our school and none of us boys can see the sence in it.

"Once a week about our teacher reads us a play by a Mr Shakespere. He does not read the real truly play but only a short resumy of it out of a book called Lamb's Tails.

"Well that made us all laufgh when we furst heard it and we called it the Lamb's Tail lesson. But we did not laughf any more when teacher said that in our homework we would have to write out our own version of the play and make remarks on it. And all on top of sums and things.

"I would not of minded if they was stories like the Deadshot Dick sereys what my father went and took away from me, but this Mr Shakespere is a pretty dull sort of a man who does not write very good English and if there is any nice or interesting persons in his plays like Miss Julia Montagu or Mr Mick Curio he goes and gets them poisoned or stabed or something before the end. And then he saves trouble by filling up his plays with common old sayings like a rose with any other name would smell the same way and other bits that I knew about since I was a kid pretty well.

* * * *

"AND now, uncle, I bet you would never gess what

idear came to me when I started to do my first Lamb's Tail home lesson.

"I thought to myself that if I just slip a peace of carbin paper under it I will have two (2) copies and then I can send uncle one and praps he might like to use it in his bits in the paper so I done that

"I have got one (1) carbin copy now of a play called Romeo and Julia pretty sloppy it is and a bit sad but some people might like it

"And now please uncle I do not want a single penny or anything for these copies. I only thought they just might be useful. So when you write tell me if you want them please uncle but if you was to offer me a million pounds I would not take it because I do not beleve my mother was right to say you were a good-natured duffer when —

"Please uncle I did not mean to write that bit, it just slipped in and I have lost my ink razer so it will have to stay but please I do not bleve one word of it

"So if you want the peaces I wrote free gratus plese let me know soon.

"Your loving nephew
"Bobby J."

P.S. — Just in case you might be intrested in wireless I mentioned I am sending inside a peace what shows the parts and price and every thing. But please send it back because in sevral years time I might be able to afford a set like that. — B.J.

Bobby wins. I wrote making a bargain with him.

ROMIO AND JULIA

Bobby J. Studies Shakespeare

IT has been said that opportunity knocks at least once at every man's door. There are certain men, however, upon whose doors opportunity is never permitted to knock, and evidence is not wanting that my very young correspondent, Bobby J., is destined to be one of them.

Long before the welcome visitor has approached within knocking range of his portals, Bobby's watchful eye will have seen him through a chink in the blind, and he will be out, halfway down the garden path, to greet the caller with flattering enthusiasm.

I have known men like that and, while I have envied them at times, I am not sure I am sorry that nature decreed I might not be numbered amongst them. Anyhow, when old opportunity comes aknocking at my front door, I am usually working — or thinking hard about working — down at the bottom of the back garden.

After I had suggested that a new wireless set might be forthcoming in payment for a number of articles on Shakespeare's plays, young Bobby, distrustful of the Postal Department, delivered his first contribution in person.

* * * *

"DEAR uncle" (he writes) "When I told my mother how you were going to give me a new wireless if I did you some bits about Mr Shakespeare the play writer my mother said I was not to take the wireless because I must have asked for it but I dident uncle did I.

"So when she writes to you like she said she would you can tell her it was absolute your own idear cant you. So please do that wont you uncle because it is the solem truth and dont you let my mother order you about as if you were nothing but a boy that reely does need a good wireless set for the tests.

"Well uncle here is my first bit which is all wrote from memry as teacher wont let us have a Shakespeare book to look at but we must do it out of our own head for homework. So you must excuse if I get a bit gumbled up sometimes because teacher has false teeth and does not speak very plain.

"Well I have decided to call it

BITS ABOUT PLAYS

By Bobby J. and Mr
Shakespeare:
No. 1 Romio and Julia.

* * * *

"WELL once upon a time there was two famlys in a town called Veroner and there was Mr Montigu's famly and Mr Capulit's family, but they wasent playing speeks at the time because of some row very likely that Mrs Montigu had with Mrs Capulit at some tennis club meeting or something like that so they both told their children they was not to speak to the other famlys children if they was to meet them in the street but just look the other way because they was not very nice people.

"Well of course young Romio Montigu, who is a bit of a softy has to go and get things all mixed up because he thinks he would like to go walking out with Julia Capulit which just shows you what sort of a chump he was to go all mushy about a silly girl.

"He dosent play cricket or football nor nothing but just loafs about under her balkiny moaning and groaning about how roses smell just the same even if you call them cabbidges and she tells him to stop swearing at the moon and — oh a whole lot of rot. This part is pretty rotten.

"Well of course they decide they got to get married so they call and see the rev Mr Laurence and he says very well come round on Tuesday and I'll marry you if you must go looking for trouble and that's what he does.

"So now there comes a bit of pretty good stuff.

* * * *

"ROMIO is walking up the street with a mate of his named Mick Curio and they run bang up against some of the Capulit fellers and then there's a pretty decent sort of a fight only not enough of it.

"First a chap named Piebald or something like that kills Mick Curio and then Romio surprises himself by killing Piebald and when he has done that of course he has to make his get away like in America so he does that.

"Well this girl Julia keeps her marriage secret and her famly want her to marry somebody else, but, of course, that would be burglary — no bigumy, and the pleece might put her in jale when they got tired of looking for Romio who is still in smoke.

"Well she goes and asks the rev Mr Laurence what about how is she going to get out of it and he says don't you worry I'll give you some special sort of asperin or something what will make people imagin you are dead but you wont be dead only asleep.

"Well, she goes to bed and takes the asperin and when they think she has kicked the bucket they put her in the toom which is a sort of upstairs grave.

"Well there she sleeps and sleeps till Romio dodges the pleece and sneeks back and finds Julia in the toom and he thinks she is dead so he sticks a knife into himself and goes dead. And the noise he makes gassing about it wakes Julia up. So she sees him there with the knife sticking out of him and gets all excited and grabs a bottle of weed killer or something what Romio had bought to spray roses very likely to make them smell different and she scoffs it and goes dead too. So they are both dead. And all I have got to say is a pretty good job too.

Bobby J., Aurther and Writer.

DOTTY MR HAMLET

"DEAR UNCLE. — My second bit about Mr Shakespeare's plays is a bit better than the first," wrote Bobby J in the covering letter of another manuscript, "because it has got a gost in it and a pretty fair lot of murders and deths and things that make it very nearly as good as a pretty good film, but not quite.

"Well the name of this story is Hamlit Prince of Denmark, but I call it

DOTTY MR HAMLIT
or
The Fella That Talked
Too Much
By Bobby J.
and
Mr Shakespeare

"And the real reason why I call it that is just because he is always talking about things in a rather dilly sort of way, but never hardly ever doing them like a real hero and a proper prince. And I don't believe he was a prince at all really because if he was he would go waving his sord and ordering people about which he hardly ever does at all but just moons about saying to be or not to be and about slinging arrows and bodkins and things.

Well as far as I can make out Hamlit's father, Mr Hamlit, senior, was once the King of Denmark, but he made the mistake one day of going to sleep under an apple tree in his orchard which is a pretty risky thing for kings to do.

* * * *

WELL while he was asleep his brother, Claude who was a bit of a crook seen him there and went and poured some poison stuff into his ear which made his blood catch alight so that he went as dead as mutton.

And the real reason Claude did this was so that he could marry Mrs Hamlit senior and get on the thrown. So that is what he did.

Well there were a lot of other people in the story who don't matter very much except Hamlit's sweetie a dilly sort of girl called O. Feelier who was the daughter of an old cove named Polony.

Well things went on and on till one night Hamlit thought he saw a gost sneaking about the back yard which just goes to show you how dippy he was really. But he followed the gost in spite of being a fair bit frightened and he said to it speak up and give an account of yourself and clergymen of grace defend us.

So the gost spins him a yarn about being his father and explains about having the stuff poured in his ear hole by Claude and he puts it up to Hamlit how about bumping off Claude for a bit of revenge and Hamlit says goodo that's what I better do I suppose, though it's going to be an awful lot of bother.

But instead of doing that Hamlit goes and gets some acters to put on a bit of a theatre show in front of the King which showed one fella pouring stuff on another fella's ear drum and when the King Claude seen that he got the wind up and says switch on the lights I'm going home because this is a pretty punk show. And he does that.

* * * *

WELL then Hamlit's mother gets hold of him to try and talk him over and Hamlit sees the window curtain move and thinks Claude is hiding there so he jabs at it with his sord and out falls old Polony stone dead.

Well Hamlit gets mooning about and he is amusing himself by having a few words with a skull in a cemetery when a funeral comes along, and it turns out to be the funeral of Miss O. Feelier (if that's how you spell it) who has gone off her dot because Hamlit chucked her and done in her father so she stuck some weeds in her hair and jumped into a waterhole and was drowned dead.

Well Hamlit goes dippier than ever after that but I didn't pay much attention to the rest except the last bit where they was having dinner one night when Miss O. Feelier's brother picks a row with Hamlit and goes for him with a poisoned sord and the King puts some more stricknin or something in Hamlet's wine and O. Feelier's brother pricks him so they are both poisoned and the queen drinks the poisoned wine by mistake and Hamlit with his dying breath stabs Claude and then a pall of Hamlit's called Hurray something wants to get poisoned too. But Hamlit says hold on if you go dead there won't be anybody left to tell Mr Shakespeare what happened so his pall says oh all right I suppose I better go on living so he does that and that's how the yarn got about.

It might have been a pretty good sort of a yarn if Hamlit hadn't kept interrupting but with everybody dead all over the shop it ended up all right.

BOBBY J.,
Writer and Orther.

BOBBY J. ON MACBETH

I FEAR greatly that the introduction of my juvenile friend, Bobby J., to the imperishable works of Shakespeare — through the medium of the expurgated versions of the excellent Charles and Mary Lamb — hardly serves to instil into a young, impressionable, but inattentive mind, a proper reverence forthe Immortal Bard.

Particularly is this so when the stories, read aloud in class, to somewhat inattentive ears, leave upon the youthful modern mind impressions greatly at variance with those desired by the teacher, however well-intentioned.

It is solely to illustrate this that I publish Bobby's naive transcripts, rather against my own inclination as a Shakespeare lover, and I feel sure, much to the annoyance of all Shakespeare societies, whose members must accept the foregoing explanation as my sole excuse.

Dear Uncle (he writes) This is a scoch story wrote by Mr Shakespeare and I reely do not think he could have known very much about Scochmen except that they are supposed to drink a lot of wisky. And this is all wrong because my father is and he dosent.

Well uncle I call this story
BOOSEY MR McBREATH
or
The Bludstained Dager
by
Bobby J. and Mr Shakespeare.

A long time ago two scoch generals named Mr McBreath and Mr Banko were motering home from a bit of a battle and they must have called in at a lot of hotels on the way because as they were crossing over a blarsted heath (Please uncle this is what teacher called it not me) when they thought they saw three ladies with beards who were whiches.

Well the whiches told Mr McBreath that he would be King of Scotland but his sons wouldn't because Mr Banko's sons would.

* * * *

WELL, Mr McBreath went home and told all about it to Mrs McBreath who dident have a very nice mind. She said it seems a funny thing to me the way you go meeting lady whiches on blarsted heaths when you are supposed to be fighting battles but all the same there might be something in what the hussies say.

Well shortly after that King Duncan the reel king thought he would spend the weekend at McBreath's place, but when he was asleep Mr McBreath killed him with a dager and blamed it on to a couple of bridegrooms.

So that's how McBreath became king over the scoch people and after he put Mr Banko on the spot and bumped him off, he thought praps he better go and have a word with the maginery lady whiches on the blarsted heath. And the whiches said to him now there's two things you got to look out for and one is a chap called McDuff who was never born but just growed up like Topsy and the other is that bit of scrub near your place called Burnem wood if it starts to walk about so you better put a bit more water in it.

* * * *

SO McBreath went home and sure enough when he looked out of a window there was a chap named McDuff outside his fence and with him was Malcom one of Duncan's sons and a lot of Diggers. And as McBreath watched he thought the bit of scrub outside started walking, and he got the wind up properly.

But of course it wasent that but just how Malcom told the Diggers to tie bits of branches on theirselves for a bit of camerflage.

So then McBreath got a bit peevish and drank a couple of wiskys and went outside and said look here do you people know you are trespasing? But McDuff said never mind that will you fight? And McBreath said of course because the whiches told me no man born could kill me.

But then McDuff said well I wasent born I just growed up and if you dont fight I will put you in a cage and sell you to a circus for a side show.

Well then McBreath got the willies again and he thought McDuff had turned into a hen so he said ha, ha, lay on McDuff. But that annoyed McDuff so he cut McBreath's head clean off with his sord and Malcom went and got on the thrown. So it ended like that a bit suddenly.

But it just goes to show you like my father says if a man goes and drinks too much wisky and cocktails and things its no good because he loses his head. So that's that.

BOBBY J.,
Orther and Writer.

BOBBY J'S MODERN OTHELLO

DEAR Uncle (writes my youthful friend, Bobby J.): If it is all the same to you I think perhaps it might be a pretty good thing to knock off these pieces by Shakespeare.

Because, Uncle, this Mr Shakespeare might have been a pretty good play-writer like people say, but I don't think he would have made much money writing for the films. He takes an awful long time to get to the exciting bits, and then they haven't got any dectectifs or master crimnals in them, nor nothing unless I put them in myself.

So please, Uncle, I think perhaps I will only do two or three more, and the one I am going to do now is one that I call

KID OTHELO
or
The Bedroom Merder
by
Bobby J. and Mr Shakespeare

Well, it seems that once there was a bit of a stuck-up flapper called Desdimoner, who liked herself so much that she turned up her nose at all the pretty decent fellas who come to see her, and said they was all just a crowd of rough necks. She said all they knew was about football and criket and they dident have any brains.

So, of course, the fellas just stopped having anything to do with her. Well she must have got pretty lonely after this, and got knocking about some pretty queer places, because pretty soon she took up with a prize fighter fella named Kid Othelo, who was a black man.

Well, he was a pretty good talker this black feller and he got skiting to Desdimoner about all the fights he'd won and how his photo was in the paper and everything, so after he got one of his seconds named Casso to put in a good word for him, what does she do but run away and marry him. I mean Othelo.

* * * *

WELL, Desdimoner's old man was pretty wild when he heard this, so he went and complained about it to Parliment, but the premier said now look here I got this Othela fella backed pretty heavy for the big fight that's coming on, so don't put him in gaol, but you better have a couple of pound on him instead and keep quiet because some of these prize fighters make a lot of money. So Desdimoner's father says all right, and he did that.

Well Othelo and Desdimoner went away to some other place where the fight was to be, but when they got there they found the other fella had not turned up and the fight was off. So they started going gay and knocking about at parties and things.

Well, Othelo had another second or trainer or something called Iago, who was a pretty nasty piece of work and terrible jelis of Casso. So what does he do but go whispering in Othelo's ear how his wife and Casso was a bit too thick, and how she had given Casso a silk handkerchief that was a wedding present from Othelo, and how they were going to the pictures together and everything.

So after Desdimoner had gone to bed one night with a headache Othelo came into the room and said Honey am you been telling me lies bout dat big boy Casso? And when she said Don't be silly Othelo said Baby Ah am gwine make you a cops. And with that he took and put a big pillow over her face and sat on it.

Well, of course Desdimoner was a bit too weak to stand much of that, so she died. And it nearly served her right for marrying a black fella.

Well, just as Othelo was straightening up the bed Casso rushed in with his face all bashed in by Iago, and he said Excuse me but that bird Iago has been telling you a lot of lies and I've got his own letters to prove it.

Well, when Othelo read the letters he said Ah been misinformed. Gee but I got dem bedroom blues! So he just took and killed himself right there alongside Desdimoner, and they had a double funeral and saved expense.

Well, there's nothing much more to tell except the police got a few clues and arested Iago and he was found gilty and strung up, and Casso had to go and look for another job, and that's that.

BOBBY J.

EPISTLES TO AB

THE FARM AND FORTUNATUS

Fourway Farm,
via Billibilli P.O.

August 2, 1934.

DEAR AB,

I am putting the full title and address of the old family seat at the top of this letter in case you might happen to forget it some time. I been told that people in the rush and bussel of city life is apt to be absent-minded in queer ways so this is just to remind you we are still at the same spot and more or less alive.

Be that as it may me and your ma was very glad to hear from you at last and to know that you are in fare health and still working at your job — or still at your job any way.

Apart from these two facks there ain't much in said letter to stir up any spechial pride in our second oldest son or raise loud cheers.

Now Ab., my boy, I don't want to spend my declining years writing these sort of letters to you. I don't enjoy it. So you got to remember it's your old man has the trouble and pain of writing them. All you got to do is read them and heed them.

Well, Ab., you will probably be pained to know we ain't sending you no five pounds in this letter such as you asked for in such a reasonable manner. In fack all the nice feasable reasons you give remine me a good bit of what I once seen a mining prospecktis. I might mention that from first to last said mine never paid no dividends.

* * * *

BE that as it may, I was a bit disappointed you should of wrote home for money so soon after settling in the city. Of course, I guessed you would sooner or later, but I was hoping it would be later — a lot later.

But you better understand, Ab., right here at the beginning, that the old blue teapot on the parler mantilpiece at this farm ain't a bit like the purse of that anscient bloke they called Fortunis or somethin'. That teapot has got a bottom, and it don't sprout no new quids inside of it every time you take one out.

Leastwise its pretty empty at present.

Well, Ab., seeing how things are I don't know as I can blame you for not taking to the land like your oldest brother Joe did. Farm life aint exackly attractive just now. When I named this place Fourways Farm years ago I done it because I reckoned I could see four ways of making a good living off it. And they was wheat sheep pigs and potaters. But the days is gone when a man could put potaters in the bank against an overdraft. And other things has slumped so as to make me think sometimes of changing the name to Noway Farm. But somewhere deep inside me I got a funny sort of faith that this bit of land will come back true to name before long.

Me and your ma been here now thirty year come next summer, and we aint blaming the land for one single thing. If human nacher and human aims was as kind and genrous as the land is this world would be a pretty fine place.

* * * *

BE that as it may, what I want to say is this. I got a sort of sispicion that betwix the lines of your letter there is indicashions you are inclined to get a bit uppitty and above yourself.

It is a frame of mind that often goes with white collars. I ain't blaming your ma one bit because she got ideas one of the famly should have a bit of schooling and be able to wear a white collar without looking like he was getting strangled by a yoke. But believe me you ain't doing my friend Mr Sprague no favor by working in his city office at three quid a week.

You might as well know first as last, Ab., that your boss Mr Sprague holds a second mortgage over the old family seat and I am finding it pretty hard to find the interest. Being a sensible man Mr Sprague seen as how I might be able to save more if I had one idle back less to clothe and one mouth less to feed that wasent so idle. So he kindly gave you a job in his office at three quid a week. And I think he'll be pretty satisfied if you manidge to earn thirty bob of it.

Well, Ab., I don't know if the sort of discontented note that runs through your letter is a sign of a great ambition or just in-growing grouch. Time alone will tell. So that will be all just now.

Love from all at home.
Your aff. father.
JAS JAMES

P.S. — Your ma is also writing.

SOME PILLS FOR THE PRODIGAL!

FOURWAY FARM,
August 6, 1934.

DEAR AB,

We received your last letter and have read it over three times to make sure there werent nothin we missed, but we have come to the conclusion that it reely must be as silly as it sounds which seems almost impossible.

Well, Ab, when you left the old family seat to go and seek fame and forchin in the great city me and your ma did wonder now and then if you would ever get nipped by any of these modern bugs. But it seems they aint been only just nipping you Ab. They been biting chunks out of you.

Be that as it may, when I tole you in my last that we would not be sending the five pounds you asked for so cheerfully I thought you would know I meant it.

That was just a plain statement of fact and I don't see there was nay call for you to swamp me under a lot of poppycock about what you call you ego and your right to self expression and living your own life.

✶ ✶ ✶ ✶

SO far as I been able to see Ab, a man's own life is the only life he has any chance of living in this world. So you go right ahead, son, and live your own life. All I got to say is you ain't going to live your life on my money. So now we got it clear.

Be that as it may, I want you to understand, Ab, that the old man still has hopes of you. And they'd be a lot stronger hopes if I was to hear that you returned to your ma that half note what she sneaked into her letter to you, when she thought I wasn't looking, out of her egg money.

It might be just as well for you to reelise that every time you blew one of them ten bobs of your ma's on one of them plucked pullets they call flappers you are spending a new hat or wot not that your ma might have had if youd give her a chance to hang on to her own egg money.

This is just a hint that's all and I'd say no more about it.

✶ ✶ ✶ ✶

BE that as it may, I am a good bit puzzled lately about the bits and scraps you put into your letters about someone you call your girl friend. This here girl friend business is a bit of a mistery to me.

If you mean that you have found some very plucky young woman willing to become your wife in ten or twenty years time when you might be able to afford to keep her me and your ma would be glad to hear about it, though I wouldent like to say you are being very fair to the girl.

Anyway, me and your ma would be a bit relieved if you was to write in plain English and let us into the secret of this here girlfriend stuff.

Well, Ab, if you have been able to let your eye wander away from the sporting collums of the newspaper you might have noticed that wheat is going up a bit. Not that it will make any difrence to you. It won't.

But I thought you might perhaps feel sort of glad that your aged parents sees signs of getting a bit of luck at last. It would make us awful pleased — speshilly your ma to know that you was pleased about something that pleased us. But I suppose modern parents has no right to become too optimistic.

* * * *

WELL, Ab, we have had a bit of rain and things is looking brighter up this way. Your brother Joe asks me to ask you if you would consider it beneath you to buy him one (1) pare of strong working boots, size 8. He will send you the money when you send the boots.

Well, Ab, I think that will be all at present.

Your aff. father,

JAS JAMES.

P.S. — Your ma is also writing.

CONCERNING DRESS SUITS

FOURWAY FARM
August 24, 1934.

DEAR AB.,

When your mother had you Christened Albert some 20 years ago, both her and me, judging by the few vage signs and indications then showing had hopes that you might turn out bright. Albert, accordin to your mother, meaning somethin bright. But since you have gone to work in a town office, Ab., I can't say as your letters bears out that hope to any startling extent.

Your latest excuse for trying to prize a fiver off the old man still leaves him calm and collected. Even the prospeck of one day beholding my second son dolled up in a dress suit don't get me terrible excited. If you feel you must have a dress suit for dances an cetra you go ahead and save up for one. But you better give up any idear of me becoming an acessary before the fack to the tune of five valuable pounds. Do I make myself plain at last?

* * * *

BE that as it may, I have lived for close up 60 years now, and I have never yet found a dress suit needful of success in me chosen way of life. Maybe in the city things is difrint, but that is entirely your pigin, my boy.

In spite of depression and droughts, I think your modest old man can claim he aint exackly made a failure of life even without a dress suit. Three times I been president of this Shire, and a councillor for close up 20 year. Durin that time I have met noomerus M.P.s. and other brass hats, I have shook hands with three Goveners and one Royal Prince of the blood. And narry a one of em, Ab, seemed to be much worried about me not owning a dress suit. No nor a top hat neether.

Even in the city, Ab my boy, you will find that the right sort of solid respeck aint to be bought with fancy clobber.

Maybe I am growing boastful with age. But altho I know people in this districk treats me pretty familier, calling me old Jim-Jim and old Jimmy Two-times-twice, still I can't help notising when a depitashun is to go to town on some serious public question, old Jimmy Two-times-twice nearly always heads the voting. Think it over, my boy.

* * * *

BE that as it may, we have received the photer you sent of the bald face young woman you call your girl friend what has probably awoke the need of dress suits. Your mother is a good bit worried, Ab. Me, I aint worrying, for I notice the said young woman, altho plucked and painted extry and above the ordinry, has a pritty shrewd and calcalating eye. I wouldent hang no hopes on that eye if I was you. Nor no imitation pearls or rabbit coats eether. Also, if them lips what looks so black in the photer is that red in reel life, I would say she is going to cost a tidy bit for renovations, repainting and generil repairs as time drifts by.

Your brother Joe, on the other hand seems to like her looks and wishes to inquire can she milk. Joe also would like you to send that (1) pare of working boots c.o.d., immedgit.

Well, Ab, I aint give up hoping one day to be able to write you a reel inthusiastick letter saying well done, my boy. What's your idears about it?

So, suspending my verdick I still remain for the time,

Your aff. father,

JAS JAMES.

P.S. — Love from all at home. Your ma is also writing, but don't go ixpecting any ½ note in her letter this time. I have shook it and put it back in the old teapot. Sorry. — J.J.

Ab.

GREAT DECISIONS

FOURWAY FARM,
August 31st, 1934.

DEAR AB. — We have received your last letter, and have took due notis of the two great decisions that you have come to. At least I suppose they are great decisions, since you have said so, and as fur as we can make out they are (1) You are thinking very serious of taking up art, and (2) As you are now 21 and have a vote, you are thinking of giving it to the Communist candidate.

Well, well.

Be that as it may. But as you don't seem to be seeking any advice from me or your ma, I don't see why you should trouble to mention these things much less write a whole letter about them.

* * * *

HOWSOEVER, if you wish me to comment on your great resolves, which I regards mainly as growing pains, all I can say concerning art is that a long line of horny-handed sons of soil on both sides of the fambly tree aint apt to perduce a genius in the painting line. But I once seen a panzy plant growing in the middle of a paddick of wheat; so a man never can tell.

As regarding your Bolshevick leanings all I got to say is that eether the old James stock is petering out and starting to get flabby about the gray matter, or else it has perduced a ideelist of sich a wonderful quality that he

Mrs James

had ought to be kept in a glass case. If you are a free and independent worker are willing to give up your liberty and good living so that remote posterity may perhaps, very likely, maybe get some probable or possable benefit out of ut, well we ought to be getting down on our knees to you and knocking our foreads on the ground.

I have read a fair bit about this subjeck, Ab, and I met one bloke what was in Russia recent, and by and large, I looks on the Australian Bolshevick or Communist as a bloke what is willing for this generation to give up a pretty fair living and deny its sons and gransons a pretty fair living in order that its great-gransons, in course of time, may perhaps win a pretty fair sort of living wot is just about as good as the sort of living their great-granfathers give up in order that their great-gransons might win it.

* * * *

I KNOW it sounds a bit mixed, but think it over, Ab.

Personal I looks on Bolshevism as a interesting but pretty dilly experiment so long as it don't come too near me.

It's like this: If I was intrested in a bloke trying to invent a pretty strong sort of high explosive it wouldent be my idear to get in the same room with him where he was doing it. I'd much rather he done his experiments in the middle of a paddick — a good big paddick — while I could sit on the fence and watch him through a telyscope.

Sich is my remarks concerning art and Communism. Your ma concurs without any added coment ixcep to say if it gits much warmer you better leave off your flannins and wear your light summer underthings. Which considering the latest simtims, strikes me as a very practical and wise remark.

Well, Ab my boy, I still hope one day to write a letter applauding some of yure scheems and idears. Meantime, with great fortishood and patience I still manidge to remain

Your aff. father,

JAS JAMES.

P.S. — Your ma and brother Joe sends their love — J.J.

LIST OF TITLES

Dates refer to the issue of the *Herald* Melbourne in which the piece was first published.